Social Needs versus Economic Efficiency in China

Sun Yefang's Critique of Socialist Economics

Social Needs versus Economic Efficiency in China

Sun Yefang's Critique of Socialist Economics

Edited and translated
with an introduction by
K. K. FUNG

Routledge
Taylor & Francis Group
LONDON AND NEW YORK

First published 1982 by M.E. Sharpe

Reissued 2018 by Routledge
2 Park Square, Milton Park, Abingdon, Oxon OX14 4RN
711 Third Avenue, New York, NY 10017, USA

Routledge is an imprint of the Taylor & Francis Group, an informa business

A Library of Congress record exists under LC control number: 82010265

ISBN 13: 978-1-138-04542-2 (hbk)
ISBN 13: 978-1-138-04546-0 (pbk)
ISBN 13: 978-1-315-17195-1 (ebk)

To John C. Pelzel
Who turned dreams into reality

K.K.F.

"To discuss politics independently of economics, to replace objective economic laws with the mass line and politics in command, and to use political explanation instead of economic explanation reflect not only the idealistic viewpoint, but also the lazy man's mentality in economics."

Sun Yefang
"Some Knowledge of Philosophy Is Necessary to Understand Economics"

Contents

Acknowledgments

1. Sun Yefang for his permission to translate Some Theoretical Issues in Socialist Economics and for his approval of my selections for the English edition.

2. Memphis State University Faculty Research Grant Fund for partial financial support.

3. Leslie Burkett, of the Bureau of Business and Economic Research, Memphis State University, for editing the Editor's Introduction and proofreading the galley of the whole volume.

4. Cyril Chang and Nancy Wulwick for their detailed comments on the first draft of the Editor's Introduction.

5. Ju Ju Fung, my ten-year old daughter, who miraculously transformed an almost illegible handwritten Editor's Introduction into a typewritten draft.

K. K. Fung
Memphis
March 1982

Editor's Introduction

K. K. Fung

I. *THEORETICAL ISSUES*—GENERAL CONTENT

Written by Sun Yefang, former director of the Institute of Economics of the Chinese Academy of Sciences, Some Theoretical Issues in Socialist Economics is a major critique of socialist economic theories and policies in China. Theoretical Issues was first published in Chinese by the People's Publishing Company, Beijing, in 1979. It contains twenty papers written over the twenty-two year period from 1956 to 1978. As Sun's positions remained remarkably unchanged over this period, there is a great deal of content duplication from one paper to another. To avoid excessive duplication, only seven papers have been selected for this English edition, representing some 40 percent of the total pages in the Chinese edition.[1]

Unlike most economic writers from China, who tend to hide their arguments behind Marxist and Maoist dogmas and escape into non sequitur whenever the logical arguments contradict those dogmas, Sun writes with an extremely lucid style, refreshingly free of these irritations.

In Theoretical Issues, Sun pointed out that existing practices of the planned Chinese economy often fell far short of official social, economic, and political objectives. He attempted to create a Marxist theoretical rationale for economic reforms in China by reinterpreting the Marxist concepts of value and the law of value. He also made policy proposals relating to the management power of enterprises, the profit target, the depreciation of fixed assets, and the allocation of producer goods.

II. SUN YEFANG—A BIOGRAPHICAL NOTE

Born in 1908, Sun studied in the USSR between 1925 and 1930. He was active in the Chinese Communist Party before the Liberation. After the Liberation, he served as deputy director of the Industry Department of East China Military and Administrative Council and as a member of its Financial and Economic Committee, president of the College of Finance and Economics in Shanghai, deputy director of the State Statistical Bureau, and director of the Institute of Economics of the Chinese Academy of Sciences. He is currently advisor to the Institute of Economics of the Chinese Academy of Social Sciences.[2]

The official publication of Theoretical Issues in 1979 typifies the political vicissitudes in China. The same papers that earned Sun the dubious reputation of being "China's biggest revisionist" and "biggest revisionist in China's economics circle" in the 1960s are now being used to justify liberal economic reforms following the downfall of the Gang of Four. But these past official stigmas and seven years' imprisonment during the Cultural Revolution only served to strengthen Sun's stature as one of China's prominent advocates of economic efficiency in resource allocation.

III. SUMMARY OF *THEORETICAL ISSUES*

A, The Importance of Value and the Law of Value

To Sun, the most fundamental theoretical issue in China was the misconceptions surrounding value and the law of value. These misconceptions were:

1. Value exists only in the capitalist economy or commodity economy.

2. The law of value operates only in the commodity economy. It regulates resource allocation through the spontaneous deviation of market prices from equilibrium prices based on value, with market prices higher than the equilibrium prices in the presence of shortages and market prices lower than the equilibrium prices in the presence of surpluses.

3. Value and the law of value operate mainly in circulation and only secondarily in production.

4. Value and the law of value still operate in socialist China because there is still exchange of commodities between the state economy and the collective economy, and within the collective economy.

5. Within the state sector, there is no commodity exchange. Value and the law of value are no longer operative.

6. If the law of value is still needed in socialist China, it is only because development among state enterprises is uneven and because commodity economy has to be developed before the communist stage can be reached. In the communist economy, commodities will cease to exist. There will be no need for value or the law of value.

According to Sun, the correct conceptions should be as follows:

1. Value is an indicator of scarcity, and the law of value governs the efficient allocation of scarce resources. Value and the law of value exist as long as scarcity exists.

2. Value is derived from the expenditure of socially necessary labor, both live and embodied.

3. Value should be based on production price (see subsection D below), an equilibrium price at which supply and demand are at long-run equilibrium when all factors of production are being compensated at their opportunity costs.

4. Value need not be realized indirectly through anarchic market exchange. Instead, it can be realized through planning.

5. Exchange and circulation still exist under socialism. But they need not be conducted through the market. Circulation will no longer realize and determine value, but instead will be directed by plan prices based on directly calculated value. Once production and circulation have been carried out according to plan prices, value will be automatically realized.

6. When supply and demand are not at long-run equilibrium, plan prices can be allowed to deviate from values to induce adjustments in production and consumption. But unlike unplanned deviations of prices from values under the market economy, planned deviations minimize the waste associated with the blind search for optimum deviations in market exchange, since the total supply and demand are known beforehand in a planned economy.

7. Concern for value is a concern for economic efficiency through optimal allocation of resources. If the law of value is not observed in economic planning, the promised superiority of socialism over capitalism can never be realized.

Sun believed that these misconceptions stemmed from confusing the forms which value and the law of value assumed in the market economy and their substance, which was applicable even in the socialist and communist economy. They represented a misinterpretation of Marx's and Engels' works. Sun was not sure whether these misinterpretations led to existing economic practices which often violated the law of value by their preoccupation with physical output (use value) rather than economic value, or whether these misinterpretations resulted from economists' attempt to rationalize existing economic practices. But he maintained that existing methods of allocating resources based on subjective wishes rather than economic value led to major economic inefficiencies.

B. The Failings of Gross Output as a Central Target

Sun thought that the use of gross output as a central criterion to assess enterprise performance led to economic inefficiency, since gross output was computed gross of multiple countings in value added at constant prices. Specifically, the following inefficiencies resulted:

1. Waste of expensive materials. The gross output targets encouraged enterprises to use expensive materials on ordinary products.

2. Unwanted inventory. In order to fulfill their overall gross output targets, enterprises were tempted to produce products with high material costs and low labor costs to balance out products with high labor content and low material costs, even when there was insufficient demand for the former.

3. Deceptive performance. When multiple countings of value added were not deducted, an increase in gross output might or might not reflect an increase in net output. Resources might therefore be misdirected if gross output alone was considered.

4. Inflated fiscal revenues. Fiscal revenues (i.e., profit delivered to the state) were calculated not according to actual sales but according to gross output. Enterprises were credited with having created a certain amount of profit once they had achieved a certain level of gross output. And the fiscal agency was correspondingly credited with having collected a certain amount of revenues. But gross output included not only output that had been sold and hence realized profit, but also unfinished products in various stages of production with unrealized profit.

C. Profit as a Substitute Central Target

Sun suggested that profit should be used instead as a central target to evaluate enterprise performance. He pointed to the following advantages:

1. Profit is simply net output net of wages. If net output is a better indicator than gross output, then profit is an even better indicator.

2. Profit reflects the annual production conditions and can help improve enterprise management. To fulfill the profit target, it is necessary to fulfill the product quantity target and to pay attention to costs and labor productivity. Therefore, although profit itself is

only a value target, material wealth will increase with the increase in profit.

3. The use of profit as a central target will force the state to adjust prices to reflect scarcity so that high profit in fact reflects better performance and not arbitrary prices.

4. The use of profit as a central target requires that the state accelerate the depreciation of fixed assets to account for invisible depreciation.

5. The use of profit as a central target also requires that the state correctly estimate the value of its fixed assets to facilitate cost accounting.

D. Prices, Capital Profit, Cost Profit, and Wage Profit

In China, plan prices were not set according to values or any other indicators of scarcity. More often than not, plan prices deviated substantially from values. As a result, profits and losses might merely reflect arbitrary prices rather than performance. According to Sun, there were two major reasons for this. The first were historical reasons. For example, the price differentials between agricultural products and manufactured goods existed before the Liberation and had not been completely eliminated. Second, economic planners had not fully accepted the principle that prices in the socialist society should directly express values. For example, low prices were set for heavy industrial products. Third, prices rather than taxes were used as a means to extract accumulation.

Sun proposed that plan prices should be set according to values. And values should be based on production prices. According to Marx, production price under capitalist production can be defined as follows:

$$(c_i + v_i) + (C_i + v_i) \times \left(\frac{s}{C + v}\right), \; i = 1, 2, \ldots, n$$

where c_i indicates the flow of constant capital (i.e., the sum of depreciation charges on fixed capital and inputs of raw materials) in value terms for the ith industry; v_i indicates the flow of variable capital, i.e., wages; s_i indicates the flow of surplus value; C_i indicates the stock of constant capital; and $C = \sum C_i$; $v = \sum v_i$; $s = \sum s_i$.

Sun called $s/(C + v)$ the capital profit rate and thought that only the capital profit rate truly represents the scarcity of constant capital. It therefore should be used to calculate production prices.

But because of the close assocation of the capital profit rate with capitalist production in the Marxist framework, cost profit rate was preferred by most Chinese economists. Prices under the cost profit rate can be calculated as follows:

$$(c_i + v_i) + (c_i + v_i) \times (\frac{s}{c + v})$$

where $c = \sum c_i$ and $s/(c + v)$ represents the cost profit rate.

There are two major differences between prices under the capital profit rate and prices under the cost profit rate. First, in calculating the cost profit rate, only the flow of constant capital is included. Fixed capital stock that has not been depreciated is excluded. Second, if s remains the same in both cases, the cost profit rate will be higher than the capital profit rate. But the profit assignable to enterprises with higher organic composition of capital (C/v) and lower turnover rate of constant capital (c/C) will be lower than that assignable to enterprises with lower organic composition of capital and higher turnover rate of constant capital, since part of the fixed capital stock that has not been depreciated is exempted from paying profit (see table on the next page).

Sun thought that using the cost profit rate to assign profit quotas to enterprises would encourage waste of scarce fixed capital. And if those economists who preferred the cost profit rate to the capital profit rate were serious about making labor the sole source of surplus value, then the wage profit rate (i.e., s/v) should be used to assign profit and calculate prices.

E. The Management Power of Enterprises

Sun criticized the overcentralization of economic management power in central government agencies and attributed the following problems to it:

1. The state was managing business that was within the scope of simple reproduction (productive capital is restored at the original value after each turnover) which the enterprise should be responsible for. For example, depreciation charges were treated as a part of state revenues. Enterprises controlled only major repair fees. Annual appropriations assigned to enterprises by the state to buy additional equipment and update technology, though not necessarily less than the capital depreciation fund sent to the state by enterprises, had to be individually applied for by enterprises and approved by the state. This restriction discouraged enterprise initiative and long-term planning on matters within the scope of simple

Table 1

Price Formation under Different Profit Rates

Industry	Constant capital (C_i) (1)	Variable capital (v_i) (2)	Used up C_i (c_i) (3)	Surplus value (s_i) (4)	s/(C + v) (II′) (5)	s/(c + v) (II″) (6)	s/v (II‴) (7)
I	95	5	10	5	.22	.37	1
II	80	20	50	20	.22	.37	1
III	60	40	51	40	.22	.37	1
Total	235	65	111	65			

	Organic composition of capital (C_i/v_i) (8)	Turnover rate of C_i (c_i/C_i) (9)	Average profit under II′ (10)*	Price under II′ (11)*	Average profit under II″ (12)*	Price under II″ (13)*	Average profit under II‴ (14*)	Price under II‴ (15*)
I	19	.1	22	37	5.6	20.6	5	20
II	4	.6	22	92	25.9	95.9	20	90
III	1.5	.9	22	113	33.7	124.7	40	131
Total			65		65		65	

Notes: Figures in columns (1), (2), (3), and (4) are in value terms. Those in columns (10), (11), (12), (13), (14) and (15) are in price terms.

s/(C + v) is the capital profit rate.

s/(c + v) is the cost profit rate.

s/v is the wage profit rate.

$s = \Sigma s_i$; $C = \Sigma C_i$; $v = \Sigma v_i$; and $c = \Sigma c_i$ where i indicates industry.

*(10) = [(1) + (2)] × (5); (11) = (2) + (3) + (10); (12) = [(2) + (3)] × (6); (13) = (2) + (3) + (12); (14) = (2) × (7); (15) = (2) + (3) + (14).

Some columns may not add up to their totals because of rounding.

reproduction, especially the renewal of fixed assets.

2. Scarce capital funds were wasted. Since all profits of state enterprises had to be delivered to higher authorities and all expenditures (except extra-quota circulating capital) were provided interest-free by the higher authorities regardless of enterprise performance, there was no incentive to earn extra profits or reduce expenditures. Enterprises all wanted to have a larger share of the funds for capital projects regardless of their economic soundness.[3]

Where state approval of fixed capital expenditures was not required, as in the case of major repairs, the appearance and basic functions of existing equipment were not allowed to be changed. The rationale was to discourage enterprises from disguising capital construction or renovation as major repairs to avoid lengthy application and approval procedures designed to guarantee funds for key projects. But this also meant that the operating efficiency of repaired equipment would be forever frozen at the original level. And it might well be cheaper to buy new equipment than to keep repairing old equipment.

3. Because the state got involved in matters within the scope of simple reproduction which should be managed by hundreds and thousands of independent accounting enterprises, it was bogged down in daily routine and was remiss in important planning for long-term national construction, namely matters within the scope of expanded reproduction and balancing the national economy.

Sun suggested that "small power" (matters relating to simple reproduction) should be given to enterprises, and "big power" (matters relating to expanded reproduction) should be reserved for government agencies. The "big power" of local enterprises should belong to local authorities, and the "big power" of Central enterprises should belong to the Central authority. And the demarcation between Central and local enterprises should be based upon the supply and marketing relationship and the coordination relationship among enterprises. With enterprises managing matters relating to simple reproduction, local authorities managing Party and mass work, and banks supervising financial management, the Central economic ministries would only have to deal with planning and research and introduction of advanced industrial technology. They would not be bogged down in routine administration.

F. Management of Material Resources

Producer goods in China were administratively allocated according to state plans because of chronic shortages. The supply and marketing relationship as well as the coordination relationship among enterprises needed to effect such administrative allocation of resources were determined and organized by the state. When such relationships were not properly organized, the following problems arose:

1. Enterprises tried to change these relationships for their own benefit and left other enterprises without alternative supply, marketing, and coordination arrangements.

2. Shortages and surpluses resulted which had to be relieved through goods-ordering conferences attended by thousands and thousands of people from different enterprises.

According to Sun, administrative allocation of producer goods among state enterprises also reflected the mistaken "natural economy" belief that there need not be any circulation of products among state enterprises under whole people ownership. This natural economy viewpoint encouraged a one-sided consideration of concrete use-value at the expense of scarcity value. As a result, allocation of resources did not observe the principle of exchange at equal values, and little consideration was given to economic efficiency.

To relieve the state from making detailed allocation decisions, Sun suggested that enterprises should be allowed to draw up periodic supply and marketing contracts and negotiate supply and marketing quantities, product varieties, and specifications without interference from the state or local authorities as long as the existing coordination relationships and supply and marketing relationships were preserved. Once contracts are drawn up, all parties to the contracts must abide by them. Any dispute should be dealt with by the planning department at a higher level.

IV. REVISIONISM OR REINTERPRETATION?

From the above summary, we can see that Sun was trying to separate the basic economic laws from the ways in which these laws had been used in the capitalist economy. He concluded that (a) scarcity value is instrumental in efficient resource allocation as long as it is realized through planning and not through market; (b) profit is acceptable as long as it does not end up in the pocket of the capitalist and reflects better performance. In other words, once the harmful distributional effects are eliminated through different institutional arrangements, the same economic laws could be used for socialist economic development.

In effect, Sun turned Marx's and Engels' works from a theory of capitalist economic development and a critique of capitalist economic practices into a theory of socialist economic development. Since Marx and Engels were not concerned with providing a detailed blueprint for economic development, Sun's efforts in this direction were extremely useful. But these apparently went against the intellectual traditions of the Chinese Marxist economists. To them, there were no common economic laws underlying both capitalism and socialism. Therefore, what was practiced under capitalism should not be practiced again under socialism. And terms, concepts, and laws that were associated with capitalism should have no place under socialism. To insist otherwise was to be revisionist.

From a non-Marxist viewpoint, we need not be concerned with the ideological purity of Sun. Nor would it be fruitful to take sides in the endless debates on what Marx and Engels did say or mean. All we need be concerned with for our present purposes is whether Sun offered a useful theory of socialist economic development.

V. PLANNING AND KNOWLEDGE

Sun contended that planning could reduce the economic waste associated with the blind search typical of market adjustments. And value could be directly realized through planning rather than indirectly validated through the market.

By planning, Sun meant some form of command planning in which the state controlled the means to enforce conformity to the plan. In order for planning to fulfill this promised superiority, the planners must know the production functions of all existing and future products, the present and future factor endowment of the economy, and the present and future preference functions of society. From this knowledge, a set of equilibrium prices and quantities can then be arrived at. In theory, if only the correct prices are announced, the economy will be able to produce the correct mix of output without detailed quantitative regulation from the planners. But unless detailed quantitative and qualitative regulations are also enforced, price signals alone will still lead to waste.

This is so because although the planners may have perfect knowledge, the producers and the consumers may not have perfect knowledge. Unless the perfect knowledge of the planners can be and is totally conveyed to the producers and the consumers, the latter must still find out through trial and error whether they belong to certain qualitative categories. Price signals and behavioral rules governing entry and exit alone cannot eliminate trial and error related to excessive or insufficient entry into a particular economic activity. For example, excessive entry in production may be owing to a lack of knowledge on the part of new entrants as to how many other competitors there are and will be. It may also be owing to an overestimation of their own ability to compete and survive in that particular activity.

For reasons of economy, it is safe to assume that the perfect knowledge of the planners will not be totally conveyed to the producers and the consumers. Therefore, waste associated with trial and error typical of market adjustments cannot be totally avoided even when perfect knowledge on the part of the planners is assumed.

If perfect knowledge is absent, the best the planners can do is to formulate some internally consistent plans for material balance based on their best estimates of the present and future production functions, preference functions, and factor endowments. But since these material balances are formulated without perfect knowledge, there is no guarantee that they will in fact be feasible given the actual functions and endowments. Even if they are feasible and internally consistent, these balances may still be technically and economically inefficient. Supporters of planning like Sun are usually attracted by the promise of internal consistency. No doubt internally consistent economic activities are neater than internally inconsistent ones. But internal consistency does not guarantee feasibility or economic efficiency.

In the absence of perfect knowledge, the most important thing is not internally consistent actions but how best to search for the needed information. Information search is generally organized in feedback loops. When a desired response is known and the goal is to maintain an established system at the desired response, the needed information is organized in a negative feedback loop. In a negative feedback loop, deviations from the desired response set in motion forces which counteract and ultimately eliminate the deviations. This is done by comparing the actual response with the desired response and executing the appropriate counteracting measures. Negative feedbacks thus stabilize the system at some chosen levels. On the other hand, when the best way to achieve a general goal has to be found or instituted, the needed information is organized in a positive feedback loop. In a positive feedback, desired (undesired) behavior is rewarded (punished), and the reward (punishment) varies directly with the extent of the desired (undesired) behavior. Positive feedbacks thus serve for loop selection, maintenance, and system expansion.[4]

The necessity of feedback loops to organize and search for information is independent of the institutional arrangements under which feedback loops perform. The only question is whether planning or market can better facilitate information organization and information search. The market is simply a particular form of a feedback system. Feedbacks can be arranged even without a market. But it is important to realize that unless a better feedback system than the market can be found, it is idle to talk about achieving greater economic efficiency. The goals of the socialist system may well be far superior, but if the socialist system must be stuck with an inferior feedback system, the superior goals may well turn into empty promises. This failure to fully realize the market as a feedback system and to properly assess the adequacy of the planned economy as a feedback system is evident in Sun's works as in the works of most socialist economists.

Without perfect knowledge, it is not very helpful to say, as Sun did, that if the correct prices are set by planning, waste associated with the price search will be reduced. The problem is that planning itself without perfect knowledge does not guarantee knowledge of correct prices.

We agree with Sun that if plan prices were set according to production prices, resources would be more efficiently allocated. When plan prices do not even cover costs of production amid chronic shortages, setting prices equal to production prices will encourage production and reduce consumption, thereby eliminating the shortages. And when plan prices greatly exceed costs of production amid surpluses, setting prices equal to production prices will discourage production and encourage consumption, thereby eliminating the surpluses. But production prices are equilibrium prices when all factors of production are only compensated at their opportunity costs. In the short run, when the market is out of equilibrium, setting some plan prices equal to production prices may not be sufficient to eliminate shortages and surpluses. In other words, in the short run, plan prices may have to be higher (lower) than production prices to increase (decrease) the supply to eliminate the shortage (surplus) before plan prices can be lowered (raised) to production prices. In fact, since costs will be different under general equilibrium, we cannot even calculate production prices which are equilibrium prices according to current disequilibrium costs.

VI. IS PLANNING SUPERIOR TO THE MARKET?

Therefore, in the absence of perfect knowledge, the difference between regulation through planning and regulation through market is not so much that planning will necessitate fewer adjustments through trial and error and consequently less waste. Rather it lies in the mode in which these adjustments are made. First, under planning, resources can be allocated through direct orders whenever price incentives are not sufficient to induce the desired allocation. Under market regulation, only price incentives can be used. Second, adjustments in prices and quantities must be coordinated and approved by a central bureaucracy under planning, whereas these adjustments can be made by individual producers under market regulation.

These differences ultimately determine whether market regulation or plan regulation is more efficient. Does the possession of coercive power make planning more efficient than the market in the allocation of resources? Where private goods providing immediate benefits with insignificant externalities are concerned, market price incentives are quite adequate to induce the desired resource allocation. Planning can do no better in this case. But where public goods and private goods with distant benefits and/or significant externalities are concerned, market price incentives are often inadequate to induce the desired resource allocation. Direct orders may be necessary. It is here that planning with its coercive power will prove to be superior to the market. Although this coercive power need not be based on public ownership of the means of production, it is definitely strengthened by public ownership. By virtue of public ownership, the state becomes the residual claimant to profits. While this permits the planners to engage freely in the provisions of goods and services with significant public goods characteristics and/or distant private benefits, it also encourages them to squeeze out market provision even where the market is efficient.

There is little advantage in centralizing changes of prices and quantities either, especially when the speed of response is of primary importance. When all adjustments of prices and quantities must be approved by a centralized bureaucracy, delays are inevitable as the applications for adjustments slowly find their way up and down through bureaucratic channels. These delays can be a major source of economic inefficiencies.

A related question is whether planning or market can better accommodate creative novelty. In an open system, creative novelty is a source of growth. But in a closed system, it is so many loose ends. Command planning with its obsession with comprehensiveness and internal consistency among targets and its monolithic bureaucracy is the epitome of a closed system. The market, on the other hand, is a quintessential open system where participants can legitimately impose uncompensated external costs on other parties through competition as long as the physical integrity of other parties' private property is not violated.[5]

The possession of coercive power, the centralization of decision-making power, and the general aversion to loose ends encouraged a form of command planning in China which cut the economy down to size to fit the primitive planning and economic management bureaucracy. Specifically, three strategies were adopted: (a) the economy was artificially simplified to reduce the number of economic linkages that need to be considered, (b) power was centralized to ensure that economic policies were implemented without deviation, and (c) feedbacks were suppressed by dissociating rewards and punishments from performance to reduce the number of adjustments that need to be made in the state plans.

The effects of these restrictive strategies resulted in (a) sectoral imbalances in the economy, (b) imbalances in budget, credit, and supplies, (c) overproduction of abundant products and underproduction of scarce products, (d) underproduction in increasing-cost industries and overproduction in decreasing-cost industries, (e) waste of capital funds, (f) economic management by administrative fiats rather than by economic considerations, (g) poor product quality, wrong output mix, and high production costs, (h) waste of manpower, (i) reduction of services and service employment opportunities, and (j) discouragement of diversity.[6]

VII. CAN THE MARKET BE AVOIDED?

Sun realized the problem of excessive reliance on quantitative control and centralized decisions. Hence, his advocacy of socialist profit as a central target and greater enterprise autonomy in investment decisions. But he failed to see the extent to which the socialist planning and economic management bureaucracy must be dismantled before the goal of economic efficiency could be realized.

For example, if profits and losses are to be used to evaluate enterprise performance, prices must be determined according to supply and demand conditions. But if prices are still determined according to production prices, they will not truly reflect opportunity costs except under equilibrium. And even if this difficulty can somehow be overcome, the bureaucratic procedures that must be gone through before prices can be changed ensure that changes will not be timely. Thus price reform necessitates two important changes in bureaucratic socialism: (a) some prices must be set by a market mechanism, and (b) price control departments should be more concerned with setting price policies than setting concrete prices. Writing at a later date, when some of Sun's proposals were being implemented, Xue Muqiao, a former director of the National Price Commission, made the following observations:

> There are hundreds of thousands of varieties of industrial and agricultural products with up to one million different prices. If market regulation is not used, the price departments alone will surely be unable to do a good regulating job. But if market regulation is to be used, the problem of reforming the whole economic management system must be faced.[7]

Later in the same paper, Xue wrote:

> We should gradually transform price departments from agencies which set concrete prices to ones that determine the direction and policies of price adjustment and supervise and guide prices.[8]

Also, enterprises can be motivated to earn higher profit only if part of the higher profit can be retained by the successful enterprises. Sun at first objected to profit retention because he thought that would be revisionist. Later, he admitted that profit retention was all right if the profit truly reflected better performance and not arbitrary prices or differential rent owing to better natural endowment. But once some profit is available for enterprises to expand reproduction, the distinction between "big power" (expanded reproduction) and "small power" (simple reproduction) becomes hazy. There is not much point in retaining profits unless enterprises can use them in ways they see fit. This means that planning has to accommodate enterprise initiatives. If this complicates command planning too much, there must be extra-plan supply sources and marketing outlets for enterprises. In other words, there must be a market among enterprises to mediate extra-plan supply and demands. And market prices generated through market allocation will inevitably put pressure on plan prices generated through administrative allocation.[9]

Although the inevitability of market allocation is clearly inferable from Sun's proposals for greater economic efficiency, Sun steadfastly resisted the market and abhorred it as a true Marxist would.

VIII. SIGNIFICANCE OF *THEORETICAL ISSUES*

Although Theoretical Issues did not have any new economic theories to offer, Sun's attempt to separate the basic economic laws governing resource allocation from the institutional arrangements under which these laws were made to function represents a significant advance in the theory of socialist economic development. Theoretical Issues also contained some of the first papers that openly and authoritatively exposed the shortcomings of the Chinese planned economy which have long been suspected by Western economists but could not be confirmed until now.

Sun's reinterpretation of the role of value in the socialist economy was all the more significant in China. Chinese economists were used to associating the concept of value and the law of value with exchange value in capitalist economies and thought that Marx and Engels predicted the disappearance of value with the arrival of socialist public ownership. Even today, more than twenty-five years after the first publication of Sun's preliminary reinterpretation and with many of Sun's proposals incorporated into current liberal economic reforms in China, there is still residual resistance among Chinese economists.

The impact of Sun's works is easily overlooked by observers today. Reading Sun's works, one might understandably mistake them as contemporary official rationalization for current economic reforms. But Sun's major points were made more than twenty-five years ago in the heyday of the three great socialist transformations of agriculture, handicrafts, and capitalist industry and commerce, when China had just successfully completed her economic recovery and the First Five-Year Plan. They even predated the reform proposals made in 1962 by the better-known Russian economist E. Liberman.

Sun's works were nothing less than heresies to the Chinese official lines. That Sun's ideas posed a threat to the regime's economic policies was evidenced by the vehement attacks aimed at him and the long jail sentence imposed on him during the Cultural Revolution. Ironically, this suppression only served to call more attention to his ideas. It is not surprising that many economists and government officials might have been secretly converted to Sun's ideas by reading his works included in the officially circulated criticism materials.

The long time lag between the publication of his major works in the late 1950s and the implementation of liberal economic reforms in the late 1970s allowed the economic practices which he criticized to thoroughly reveal their predicted inadequacies. It also gave time for his ideas to germinate in the minds of economists and government officials. When liberal economic reforms finally came, less time was needed to fight the ideological battle, as it had begun long before and was already partly won.

It is difficult for people living in a more open society where ideas can be freely expressed at little personal cost to appreciate the importance of Sun's radical ideas. In a closed society like China, where everybody tends to speak the same ideological tongue and access to mass media is tightly controlled, radical ideas cannot be tolerated and are generally suppressed with heavy-handed measures. Anyone who speaks out against the official lines must therefore be prepared to pay a high price. It is interesting to speculate whether Sun was fully aware of the high price that he might have to pay for speaking out against the official lines. If he was, his personal courage is all the more admirable. Even if he was an unwitting victim of his frankness, his personal sacrifice is no less real, and the indebtedness of China's socialist cause to him is no less deserved. Perhaps this great personal sacrifice was unavoidable, given the seriousness of the issues at hand. If the same points had been raised by an economist of lesser stature, they might never have been published and noticed. Consequently there would be no need for punishment and little personal sacrifice. For these points to have produced an impact, they had to be made by an economist with Sun's stature. And therefore severe punishment and great personal sacrifice were all but inevitable.

NOTES

1. See Appendix for contents of the Chinese edition.
2. Wolfgang Bartke, Who's Who in the People's Republic of China (Armonk, N.Y.: M. E. Sharpe, Inc., 1981), p. 338.
3. See also Xue Muqiao, Current Economic Problems in China, edited and translated by K. K. Fung (Boulder, Colorado: Westview Press, 1982), pp. 77, 78n, and Editor's Introduction.
4. For a more detailed discussion of negative feedback, see Man and His

Technology — Engineering Concepts Curriculum Project, Polytechnic Institute of Brooklyn (New York: McGraw-Hill Book Company, 1971), Chapter 7, "Feedback." For a discussion of positive feedback, see M. Maruyama, "The Second Cybernetics," American Scientist, vol. 51, 1963, pp. 164-79.

5. For a detailed discussion of closed and open systems, see K. K. Fung and Allan C. Deserpa, "Limits to Growth through Functional Specialization in a Closed System," Social Science Quarterly, vol. 59, no. 2, 1978, pp. 274-83, and K. K. Fung, "On Romantic Love — An Analysis of Open System Behavior," Policy Sciences, vol. 11, no. 2, 1979, pp. 179-86.

6. Xue, Current Economic Problems in China, Editor's Introduction.

7. Ibid., p. 65.

8. Ibid., p. 77.

9. Ibid., pp. 67, 70.

Social Needs versus Economic Efficiency in China

Sun Yefang's Critique of Socialist Economics

Author's Preface

Sun Yefang

With the exception of the last four, all the papers in this collection were all written before the Cultural Revolution. And most of them have not been published for the public before. But on the eve of the Cultural Revolution, when Chen Boda was the editor of Hongqi [Red Flag], most of these papers were included in Neibu weidinggao [Internal Drafts] published by Hongqi's editorial department as criticism materials. During the Cultural Revolution, they were reprinted as Pipan cailiao [Criticism Materials] in some parts of the country. The papers in this collection were mostly based on the four volumes of Neibu weidinggao reprinted in Shanghai.

I must thank a comrade in Hongqi's editorial department. When Chen Boda ordered him to delete and change parts of my papers for publication in Neibu weidinggao as criticism materials, he did not follow his order. Instead, he printed them in their original form and, furthermore, he addressed me as "Comrade Sun Yefang" in his "Editorial Comments." Therefore, not only was he reprimanded by Chen Boda then, he was also criticized for this later on during the Cultural Revolution.

Second, I must thank an old comrade-in-arms in Shanghai. She ran the risk of inviting criticism during the Cultural Revolution by preserving these four volumes of Neibu weidinggao reprinted in Shanghai. She also sent them to me as a gift in 1976 to celebrate my release from prison before the "Gang of Four" was exposed (I was imprisoned for more than seven years by Chen Boda and the "Gang of Four" during the Cultural Revolution for an unspecified crime). Finally, I must thank many comrades in the Institute of Economics for preserving at their own risk the several papers that were not included in Neibu weidinggao (with the exception of "We Must Have a Complete Understanding of Chairman Mao's Discussion on the Law of Value"). My papers (including Neibu weidinggao), whether they were kept by the reference office of the Institute of Economics or kept by private individuals, were supposed to have been destroyed according to the order from above. I must especially thank comrades Lin Qingsong and Lin Quanshui in the Institute of Economics. They are primarily responsible for editing this collection and gathering some papers.

Even in 1964, that is, two years before the Cultural Revolution, Chen Boda had already convicted me on the basis of the papers included in Neibu weidinggao as "China's biggest revisionist." Later on, Lin Biao, Chen Boda, and the "Gang of Four" again "crowned" me on the basis of these papers as the "biggest revisionist in China's economics circle." In these papers, I proposed to "build planning and statistics on the law of value." I also said, "among all laws, the law of value is the most important"; I emphasized the importance of the circulation process in the socialist economy and even in the future communist economy; I proposed in my research report "The Profit Target in the Management System of the Socialist Planned Economy" that, provided that prices were determined according to production prices[a] and other conditions were fulfilled, profit was a comprehensive target for evaluating enterprise performance; I proposed to expand enterprise power by decentralizing decision-making on depreciation and renovation of fixed assets. Because of these above views, Lin Biao, Chen Boda, and the "Gang of Four" accused me of advocating "revisionist profit in command" and "revisionist enterprise independence."

Such socialist economic categories and management principles as the law of value under the socialist planned economy, socialist profit, and greater enterprise power that were advocated in these papers are now increasingly accepted by practitioners in finance and economics and researchers in economic theory. But the purpose of republishing these papers is not to show how correct I have been and that the viewpoints in these papers are "100 percent correct." There is no such thing as being "100 percent correct." On the contrary, I criticized myself in "Pursue Socialist Profit with Confidence" (included in this collection) as follows:

Under the influence of the "communist fever" fanned up by Chen Boda and Zhang Chunqiao which opposed "material incentives" and rejected the prin-

a) See Editor's Introduction and Chapter 6 in this volume. — K.K.F.

> ciple of distribution according to labor, I generally opposed the bonus system and profit retention in enterprises in my 1963 paper "The Profit Target in the Management System of the Socialist Planned Economy." I favored delivery of all enterprise profit to the state with no retention at all. This position is wrong and "detrimental to production increase."

And [I criticized this as] "Left thinking." But these are merely erroneous ideas that I had detected myself; there may be other erroneous ideas that I have not detected. More importantly, even if the basic points in some papers are correct, are all my arguments completely valid? For example, nobody now still regards the law of value in the socialist planned economy as a law of the capitalist economy, or the law of value as revisionist. But whether it is an economic law that applies only when commodity exchange still exists, or whether, as I have insisted, the law of value applies as long as large-scale social production exists, remains a question. Or, even if the law of value is an objective economic law that must be respected, is it appropriate to say "build planning and statistics on the law of value"? Questions such as these are far from settled in the economics circle and require further study.

During the Cultural Revolution, even though I was criticized twice in national newspapers and magazines under the orchestration of Lin Biao, Chen Boda, and the "Gang of Four," the above-mentioned theoretical points were not touched on at all. As to my "Left" objections to the bonus system and profit retention by enterprises, for obvious reasons they were even less criticized. Therefore, the primary purpose of my publishing these old papers is to stimulate discussion among practitioners in finance and economics on the theoretical points raised in them and to solicit criticism. I will continue to study these questions with comrades in the economics circle for the sake of seeking truth and correcting errors. Even though I do not think that my theoretical points are or can be "100 percent correct," I sincerely believe that the questions raised in these papers are important practical problems presently confronting socialist economic construction; they consequently are also important theoretical questions in political economy. Therefore, a resolution of these controversial questions is not only extremely important for practical work but also for theoretical research. I hope the publication of this collection can stimulate discussion on these points among the economics circle.

Finally, I must mention one thing in passing here. In the forum convened by the Chinese Academy of Social Sciences to expose and criticize the "two sets of estimates" fabricated by the "Gang of Four" (see Renmin ribao [People's Daily] , March 16, 1978, p. 3), I mentioned a report on accumulation rate that I had written in 1963. This report is not included in this collection, for it is missing. The reason that it is missing is because some points in this report were considered useful by comrade Li Fuchun, the late vice-premier and director of the State Planning Commission. He even made margin comments on this report. When Chen Boda predetermined that I was the "biggest revisionist" in 1964, Comrade Li Fuchun was still in charge of the State Planning Commission. Therefore, this report was not included in Neibu weidinggao. This is another incidence of what is called "benefiting from misfortune" and "suffering from good fortune." If Chen Boda did not include some of my papers in Neibu weidinggao as "criticism materials," they would have been destroyed like many other research reports and unpublished papers. The research report on accumulation was luckily excluded as "criticism materials" because comrade Li Fuchun thought highly enough of it to make margin comments on it. But it was exactly because of this that it has not been preserved. Because the issues raised by this report still have practical relevance now, I will talk briefly about its content here.

At the national conference on planning convened at Baidaihe in 1963 (or 1962), many speakers analyzed the reasons for the big difficulties in the previous three years. Apart from natural disasters, contract violations, and withdrawal of technical experts by Khrushchev, another contributing factor was thought to be the excessively high accumulation rate. It was claimed that the accumulation rate should not exceed 25 percent of national income, and so on.

I wrote a report for Comrade Li Fuchun on this matter. I used mathematical formulae to prove that: if the growth rate of the consumption fund does not exceed the growth rate of agricultural output (e.g., both may be 5 percent), and the growth rate of industrial output exceeds the growth rate of agricultural output (e.g., 15 percent), and all of the excess of the growth rate of industrial output over the growth rate of agricultural output and consumption fund is invested to expand reproduction, then the accumulation rate might exceed 25 percent of national income for an extended or short period of time without affecting the annual improvement of people's living standard and the normal development of production. (Suppose the growth rate of agricultural output and the growth rate of the consumption fund were both 5 percent, and the growth rate of population was 2 percent, then three percentage points from the growth rate of the consumption fund could be used to improve people's living standard.) I thought that the big difficulty in the previous three years was also owing, apart from the above-mentioned reasons, to the phony nature of fiscal revenues. The real revenues were in fact inadequate to support such high accumulation rates. The phoniness of fiscal revenues was not only manifested in inflated growth rates of industrial and agricultural output, but also in the unscientific method of calculation. Our fiscal revenues (i.e., profit delivered to the state) were not calculated according to actual sales but to gross output.[b] The enterprise was credited with having created a certain amount of profit once it had completed a certain level of gross output. And the fiscal agency was correspondingly credited with having collected a certain amount of revenues. But gross output not only included output that had been sold and hence realized profit, but also products in various stages of finishedness with unrealized profit. At the end of the 1950s and in the beginning of the 1960s, this portion of unrealized output and profit was very substantial because of the single-minded pursuit by enterprises of gross output. Gross output also included idle inventory, a large part of which might be defective or useless. When the exaggeration fever was in vogue, such idle inventory was very substantial. Thus the phoniness of fiscal revenues.[c] Comrade Li Fuchun valued my report highly and asked me to discuss this problem with representatives from fiscal agencies who were attending the conference on planning. But they all disagreed with my views and claimed that the shortcomings that I alluded to have long been overcome by the fiscal agencies. Thus nothing ever came of this "study."

November 6, 1978

b) See Chapter 2 in this volume. — K.K.F.

c) For the connection between idle inventory and bank loans, see Xue Muqiao, China's Socialist Economy (Beijing: Foreign Languages Press, 1981), pp. 191-93. Also Xue Muqiao, Current Economic Problems in China, ed. and trans. by K. K. Fung (Boulder, Colorado: Westview Press, 1982), Editor's Introduction. — K.K.F.

1

Build Planning and Statistics on the Law of Value

For a long time, people have been saying that the law of value is a category belonging to the commodity economy; that it is in opposition to the socialist planned economy; and that the wider and deeper the scope of planned management, the more limited will be the influence of the law of value. They argue that if value still performs any function in the socialist society, it is only because there still exists collective ownership and individual ownership outside the state economy under whole people ownership. Therefore, commodity exchange still exists among these ownership systems, and wages for staff and workers are still paid in the form of money. That is to say, in the future communist society with a single whole people ownership, the law of value will be useless. And even in the socialist society, the law of value is not an objective law in the production process of its most basic ownership system (i.e., whole people ownership or state economy). It results only from the exchange relationship which the whole people ownership system has with other ownership systems. It belongs to the circulation process. Therefore, the law of value need not be considered, at least in the production sphere of state enterprises.

To clarify our problem, we must first explain what Marx's law of labor value is and how this law functions in the commodity economy. We will explain this from two aspects.

First, Marx's theory on the law of value tells us: In the commodity economy, the value of any commodity is created by labor. Therefore, the value of commodities is determined by the labor consumed in producing them, i.e., labor time. But this does not mean that the poorer the working conditions are, the more backward the technology is, and the more unskilled the worker is, the higher will be the value. Commodity value is not determined by the labor time of individual workers, but by the average socially necessary labor time. Therefore, labor expended by the unskilled worker whose working conditions are poor, and whose technology is backward, will be higher than the average socially necessary labor. As a result, he makes very little money or may even suffer loss. He may even be eliminated in the long run if he does not change. On the other hand, if the individual labor consumption of the producer is lower than the socially necessary labor, he will earn extra profit and his business will prosper. To make his business prosper, or at least to avoid loss and elimination, the commodity producer constantly thinks of ways to improve technology and management. In this way, the law of value constantly compels progress in production much like a merciless whip. In his Communist Manifesto, Marx said that the capitalist society awakened the tremendous productive capacity of social labor from its deep slumber as though by magic. In less than 100 years, it had created a productive capacity much greater than the sum total of that created in the previous ages. This magic is none other than the law of value which exerts its spontaneous influence through competition. That is to say, the law of value propels technological improvement and development of productive capacity in the commodity economy.

Second, competition exists not only among enterprises within one production department, but also among production departments. Because commodity production is blind and spontaneous, supply and demand can never be in equilibrium, and market prices fluctuate continually around values (socially necessary labor). Amid these price fluctuations, some commodity producers in some production departments make windfall profits, while other commodity producers in other production departments go bankrupt. Amid these price fluctuations, those who can survive and develop are those enterprises that can continually improve technology and management. But competition among production departments, like competition within the same department, not only propels technological improvement and development of productive capacity, it also diverts social capital and labor power from one production department to another. The law of value thus performs its spontaneous function as a regulator of production and a distributor of social productive capacity.

Now let us see if the law of value as it was described above can still play a role in the socialist society, particularly in the communist society.

First, commodities are a historical category. In the communist society, there will no longer be commodity exchange. Products are no longer commodities. The direct purpose of social production is for use value and not value. These principles can all be affirmed. But whether they are called products or directly called use value, they are still created by labor or they can be said to have been secured at the cost of a certain amount of labor consumption. This cost is of course not an end, but only a means. But it still does not change the nature of the issue. Cost must be calculated whenever it is incurred. Whether this cost is called "value" or directly "average socially necessary labor" is not that important.[a]

Second, in the commodity economy the law of value itself becomes a spontaneous, yet extremely sensitive, automatic calculator that calculates the average socially necessary labor in products. It constantly reminds backward producers to improve their work or suffer severe punishment. It also constantly encourages advanced producers to push forward by giving them handsome rewards. It is impartial in meting out rewards and punishment.

In the socialist and communist societies, we restrict or eliminate the destructive effects of market competition. This is good. But we cannot do away with calculating the average socially necessary labor of products. A denial or underestimation of the influence of the law of value in the socialist economy is in effect a denial of the importance of calculating the average socially necessary labor. As a result of this denial, our planning and statistical targets emphasize physical quantities and neglect values. They emphasize production results (i.e., "gross output") and neglect to analyze the composition of these results (i.e., the proportions of newly created value versus transferred value; or, equivalently, the proportions of net output versus material consumption). They pay even less attention to analyze how labor productivity can be improved by calculating average socially necessary labor and hence ultimately achieving the goal of higher material wealth.

Although we have many planning and statistical targets such as the seven targets for enterprise managers (namely, gross output, commodity output, product quantity, labor productivity, cost, profit,

---

a) This point is taken up again in Chapter 3 in this volume, p. 46, pp. 53–54, pp. 65–66. — K.K.F.

and circulating capital), our major target under the present planning system and management system is "gross output" at constant prices. That is to say, it is a physical target. It is not a comprehensive target in the whole system of targets. It cannot lead other targets. The fulfillment of the "gross output" target often conflicts with the fulfillment of other planning targets. "Gross output" is not an important lever for improving enterprise financial management.

Denying or underestimating the functions of the law of value amounts to denying the need to transform backward enterprises through calculating average socially necessary labor. We know that in agriculture the value of agricultural products is determined by labor consumption on the marginal land (i.e., the maximum consumption, and not the average socially necessary consumption). This is determined by objective natural conditions (the limited supply of land). This is the origin of differential rent. At present, prices of industrial products are also determined by labor consumption in the most backward plants so that they can continue to produce.[b] But what is the advantage of this policy other than perpetuating backwardness? (Of course, the "differential profit" resulting from these prices is a source of our accumulation. But must accumulation come in this form? Why can't other forms, such as taxation, perform the same function?) To let backward plants continue to produce, it is necessary to help them to improve technology and the management system. The staff and workers of these enterprises, particularly their leaders, must be constantly reminded that their labor consumption already exceeds the average socially necessary labor. We should not comfort them with a backward quota.

The capitalist never forgets this law of value based on average socially necessary labor, not even in his dreams. Sometimes, it turns into a devil threatening the capitalist with loss and bankruptcy. Sometimes it turns into abnormal profit and abundant affluence, luring him onward like a seductive siren. Whatever the forms this law happens to assume, it always compels the capitalist to go ever forward. It is inconceivable to the capitalist to produce without calculating costs. But it seems to us that the right spirit is to build socialism "at all costs." We seem to be so mesmerized by such

b) According to neoclassical economics, rent whether in agriculture or in manufacturing arises always from nonhomogeneity of factors of production given certain demand conditions. For the marginal firm earning zero economic profit, its average economic cost at its profit maximizing output level is always the highest among the producing firms in the industry. — K.K.F.

negative pronouncements as "value and the law of value are categories belonging to the commodity economy!"; "capital, profit, etc., are capitalist concepts!"; "bourgeois viewpoints," etc. that we often dare not dwell on the issues involved.

Admittedly, the law of value is a blind and spontaneous law in the commodity economy. There, it is associated with such negative factors as market competition, economic crises, unemployment, as well as colonial plunders and wars of aggression. Under the socialist system, we have transformed this blind and spontaneous law into a law subject to our conscious control. Consequently, we have eliminated its negative and destructive aspects and retained and extended its constructive aspects.

Not only should we not exclude the use of the law of value (by calculating the average socially necessary labor) to aid the development of social productive forces in the socialist society, but we should value it highly.

The secret to developing production is to lower the average socially necessary labor, improve technology, improve management methods, make labor consumption (including live and embodied labor) in the few backward enterprises catch up with the majority medium enterprises, make the majority medium enterprises catch up with the few advanced enterprises, and further improve the performance of the few advanced enterprises. Constant emulation among the backward, the medium, and the advanced enterprises to lower the level of average socially necessary labor is the broad avenue to develop production and increase social wealth.

The bourgeoisie does not accept Marx's labor theory of value. But the capitalist uses this law well in his practice. For whether the law of value is accepted or not, it exerts its spontaneous influence (to propel production and regulate productive forces) through market competition in the commodity economy. We worship Marx's labor theory of value, but we want to excommunicate this theory together with the free market from the socialist regime. The law of value becomes less active when the free market does not exist or when it is under restraint, but it still exists. Therefore, we should all the more value it, search for it, discover it, respect it, and further master it so as to make it serve us. Otherwise, it will punish us more severely than it punishes the capitalist.

Now let us see if the other aspect of the above-mentioned law of value, namely the function of regulating production, or the function of distributing social productive forces, still exists in the socialist economy. In the past, it was thought that in the socialist society the law of value performed certain regulating functions only within the sphere of commodity circulation. In the production sphere, the law of value no longer performed any regulating function. And it could not regulate the allocation of labor among the various production departments. When the second stage of the communist society was reached, and after commodity circulation had been completely eliminated, the law of value would wither away as a historical category and would not perform any regulating function in any sphere. The allocation of labor would then not be regulated by the law of value, but by the social needs for products. The strongest evidence to support this position seems to be: in a socialist country, the industry that is to be wholeheartedly developed is not the more profitable light industry, but the less profitable or even unprofitable heavy industry. The distribution of productive forces or the distribution of investment are to be determined by the state planning agencies in accordance with given policies.

But we must first ask: Why in the socialist country is heavy industry less profitable than light industry, or even unprofitable? There are only two reasons why an enterprise is unprofitable: (1) the enterprise is itself poorly managed; (2) prices are not rational. We cannot accept that heavy industrial enterprises are generally more poorly managed than light industrial enterprises. Therefore, the only reason why heavy industrial enterprises are less profitable or unprofitable is the second reason mentioned above — prices for heavy industrial products are unreasonable, namely, they are generally lower than those for light industrial products. Therefore, this is not the reason for objecting to the law of value as a regulating device. Rather, it proves that this is the adverse result of violating the law of value in the price policy.

Second, it is also one-sided to claim that the allocation of labor among various production departments within the whole people ownership economy or in the second stage of the communist society will not be regulated by the law of value, but only by the social need for products. The need for products represents only one side of the story. The other inseparable part is: If the labor productivity in producing a certain product increases, then the need for labor in this production department, or equivalently the amount of investment, will be reduced relatively or even absolutely.

Therefore, judging from the basic content of the above-mentioned law of value, we can safely assume that this law will continue to exist and perform its function both in the elementary stage and in the most advanced stage of the communist society. The only difference is the form of this function and the form in which this law manifests itself. In the commodity economy, it performs its function and manifests itself through commodity circulation and market competition. Therefore, it is destructive in nature. In the planned economy, we should actively ascertain it through calculation.

In fact, these are not the original ideas of any contemporary person. The following passage from Marx's Capital carries the same message as the one above:

> After the abolition of the capitalist mode of production, but still retaining social production, the determination of value continues to prevail in the sense that the regulation of labor-time and the distribution of social labor among the various production groups, ultimately the bookkeeping encompassing all this, become more essential than ever.[1]

It should be pointed out that the bookkeeping mentioned in the above quotation from Marx should be understood in its broad sense as to include statistics, accounting, and technical business calculations.

Why was this important revelation of principle by Marx ignored by the theorists in the past? It is difficult to say whether our now much criticized planning and statistical methods and value-independent price policy result from our negating or underestimating the function of the law of value in the socialist economy because we have forgotten this important revelation of Marx, or whether we have ignored Marx's important revelation and claimed that the law of value will wither away in the socialist society exactly because we have adopted such practices. Theory and practice often affect one another. For our present purposes, the important thing is to criticize extensively the position that claims that the law of value no longer plays a role in the socialist economy so that our practice can be changed. To negate or underestimate the function of the law of value in the socialist economy can bring only harm. On the other hand, only good will come to our socialist construction if we accept and emphasize the function of this law and respect it in our practice.

Of course, more quotations from Marx's and Engels' works can be found that seem to support an opposite position. For example, Marx said in his Critique of the Gotha Program:

> Within the co-operative society based on common ownership of the means of

production, the producers do not exchange their products; just as little does the labor employed in the products appear here as the value of these products, as a material quality possessed by them, since now, in contrast to capitalist society, individual labor no longer exists in an indirect fashion but directly as a component part of the total labor.[2]

Engels also said in his Anti-Duhring: "Direct social production and direct distribution exclude ... the transformation of products into values."[3]

How can these quotations from Marx and Engels be reconciled with what Marx said in Capital, quoted above, that "the determination of value continues to prevail" in a society under whole people ownership? Are there contradictions between these two positions?

I think that these contradictions, if any, are superficial ones.

It should first be pointed out that when Marx talked about "just as little does the labor ... appear as the value" in Critique of the Gotha Program and Engels said that "exclude the transformation into values" in Anti-Duhring, they were talking about value in connection with commodity exchange and the contradiction between social and individual labor. Their purpose was to prove that in a society under public ownership, the labor of each member directly became a part of social labor and did not need to await validation from the market when his products were sold. Therefore, Marx used the phrase "just as little ... appear," and Engels used the phrase "exclude ... transformation." The important words here are "appear" and "transformation." That is to say, when Marx and Engels talked about value here, they were talking about the exchange relationship and exchange value rather than the substance of value. And when Marx talked about "the determination of value continues to prevail" and "the determining factor of value," "value" and "value determination" actually referred to the substance of value.

Of course, I dare not say that I have correctly understood these statements by Marx and Engels. I hope that my colleagues in theoretical research will study in depth Marx's and Engels' works relating to the essence of this question. But, I think we can be certain of one thing. That is: Marx's and Engels' works on political economy were primarily concerned with capitalist commodity economy. Often, they mentioned economic laws in precapitalist society only for the purpose of explaining the laws of capitalist commodity economy. They talked even less about the economic laws in the future communist society. This is the major distinguishing characteristic between socialist theory and utopian socialism. We cannot ask Marx and Engels to prophesize at their time too much about economic laws in the future communist society. Among the analyses of economic laws in the future society, one point was entirely certain and clear. That is: All things associated with private property, commodity exchange, and free competition, namely the special forms in which the law of value manifests itself in the commodity economy, will no longer exist with the disappearance of commodity exchange. But they never said in their works that the calculation of socially necessary labor as the substance of value, and its regulating and controlling functions, will lose its meaning in the communist society.

On the contrary, in the above quotation from Marx's Capital, volume 3, Marx clearly pointed out that "the determination of value continues to prevail" in regulating labor time and distributing social labor among various production groups. Also, it would "become more essential than ever." Marx did not say the "law of value," only "the determination of value." But can this choice of terms have such pivotal importance?[c] Marx emphasized the determination of value in a certain sense. That is to say, it is no longer the "determination of value" in a commodity economy. But "determination of value" is still "determination of value"!

Many people still remember that there was a big dispute over the object of political economy among Marxist economists about thirty years ago. At that time, some people thought that Marx's works on political economy dealt essentially with the commodity economy, especially the capitalist commodity economy. They analyzed that production relationships between man and man were concealed behind things (commodities). Therefore, it was thought that once private property was abolished, and commodity economy eliminated, the production relationship between man and man could then be directly manifested without going through the relationship between commodity and commodity. And political economy as a science would disappear owing to the disappearance of its object of study. We all know that this position was later criticized. The correct interpretation is: political economy not only studies the production relationships and economic laws of commodity economy, it also studies the production relationships and economic laws of all societies. At first, many people divided political economy into the narrow sense and the broad sense. Now this distinction is no longer

c) This point is taken up again in Chapter 3 in this volume, pp. 60-61.— K.K.F.

used. For this division is basically unsound.

The present views regarding the "law of value" are similar to the view of many years ago regarding political economy itself. At first, it attempted to associate the fate of the law of value with the fate of the capitalist economy, or at most the commodity economy. At present, it appears that the law of value will exist longer than we ever expected. But should we make a distinction between the "broad sense" and the "narrow sense"? Or should we follow Marx to distinguish between the law of value "in this sense" and the law of value "in that sense"? It appears that these are also unnecessary. The law of value is the law of value. As to in what forms this law manifests itself and how it performs its functions in different societies, these should be studied and explained by political economy as a science.

Since we admit the law of value still performs its functions in the socialist society or even in the communist society, a further question can be raised: How can the law of value be related to Stalin's famous basic law of the socialist economy? That is, "to guarantee the maximum satisfaction of society's material and cultural needs by constantly increasing and improving socialist production on the basis of advanced technology." And how can it be related to the law of planned and proportional development of the socialist national economy?

Let us talk about the first question first. Another way of putting this law of Stalin's is this: To generate maximum satisfaction of social need by greatly developing labor productivity. To maximally satisfy social needs is the task and goal of developing the socialist national economy. To develop greatly labor productivity is the means to achieve this goal. But to develop greatly labor productivity, it is necessary to master the law of value.

In the past, because the significance of the law of value in the socialist economy was negated or underestimated in theory, it was thought that the direct goal of developing the national economy in the socialist society was to satisfy social needs maximally. And material wealth rather than value was thought to be relevant to this goal. Consequently, physical targets rather than value targets were emphasized in planning and statistics. Obviously, this was a one-sided view.

Use value and value, to create more material wealth with the same quantity of labor and to create the same amount of material wealth with a lower consumption of average socially necessary labor, are one and the same thing, or two aspects of the same process. They cannot be separated. Neither one of them can be ignored. To pay more attention to value and the calculation of labor consumption in planning and statistical methods is to promote the development of productivity. This is entirely compatible with the goal of producing more material wealth.

Let us now consider how the law of value can be related to the planned and proportional development of the national economy. We can be certain that the law of value is not incompatible with the planned management of the national economy. Nor are those two laws unrelated to each other. The planned and proportional development of the national economy must be built upon the law of value. Those economic policies (including price policy) and economic plans that ignore the law of value and reflect merely subjective wishes will end up disrupting all proportional relationships and hindering the rapid development of the national economy.

Only by building planning on the law of value can plans be realized and can the advantages of planning be fully exploited. Therefore, statistical workers should not limit their jobs merely to inspecting the implementation of national economic plans. They should put more efforts into mastering the law of value and tapping potentials to develop the national economy. In concrete terms, statistical work should not only be concerned with statistics on output level, namely calculating material wealth, but also the calculation of value in material production. In other words, more attention should be paid to calculating and studying costs and labor productivity; more attention should be paid to formulating national economic balance tables and calculating and studying national income; and more attention should be paid to studying the proportional relationship between national income and fiscal revenues and the proportional relationship between production, accumulation, and consumption. Only by doing these can statistics more fully serve planning and enterprise management and can the functions of planning and statistics be more fully exploited.

POSTSCRIPT

This paper is part of a manuscript based on several talks by this author at a conference convened by the State Statistical Bureau to study planning and statistical targets. Therefore, the original purpose was not to explain the complete functions of the law of value in the socialist economy. Rather, this basic issue was mentioned merely to explain some targets and methods in planning and statistics. Also, because of my prolonged lack of practice in political economy, this paper inevitably suffers from logical looseness and other errors. I publish this paper here at the suggestion of the editor of Jingji yanjiu [Economic Research] in order to solicit constructive criticisms and in the hope that this issue will be discussed more widely.

On Engels' birthday, November 28, 1956
Jingji yanjiu, 1956, No. 6

NOTES

1. Marx, Capital, volume 3, People's Publishing Company, 1966, p. 1000. [English translation based on the English edition published by Progress Publishers, Moscow, 1959, volume 3, p. 851. – K.K.F.]

2. Marx, Critique of the Gotha Program, People's Publishing Company, 1955, p. 19. [English translation based on the English edition edited by C. P. Dutt and published by International Publishers, New York, 1938, p. 8. – K.K.F.]

3. Engels, Anti-Duhring in Complete Works of Marx and Engels, volume 20, People's Publishing Company, 1971, pp. 333-34. [English translation based on the English edition translated by Emile Burns and published by International Publishers, New York, 1939, p. 337. – K.K.F.]

2

"Gross Output" and Related Issues

Some heated discussions have been started around ways to improve the methods and systems of planning and statistics. There are two aspects to this problem: one relates to the planning system itself; the other equally important aspect relates to the targets and methods of planning and statistics. These two aspects are closely related and cannot be separated.

For example, with respect to the planning system, we favor big planning and small freedom, and oppose excessively centralized planning. What does this mean? Simply put, it is a question of which targets to control and which targets to let go. The targets that the Central agencies, especially the State Planning Commission and State Economic Commission, should control are those that are the most central among the whole system of targets. Once these are controlled, all the other targets will fall into place. Those targets whose management is decentralized to various ministries, bureaus, enterprises, and local Party and government organs are not necessarily unimportant. On the contrary, among the targets that are managed by different organizations at different levels, there may be some very important ones. But they are not comprehensive targets and cannot play a leading role. Or we may say that exactly because some targets are too important, they must be jointly managed at different levels. If they are managed solely at the Central level by the planning agencies, they may suffer from inflexibility.

Therefore, the problem of big planning and small freedom is not merely a problem of the planning system, but also a problem of planning targets and planning methods. The guiding principle governing the planning system has long been established (namely, appropriate decentralization rather than excessive centralization); but the concrete problems regarding what targets should be controlled and what targets should be let go has not been solved. If this problem regarding targets is not solved, then we will be constantly worried about controlling too much or letting go too much. In other words, there is no definite idea about what should be planned and what should be free.

Here we are mainly concerned with this problem regarding targets and methods.

CAN GROSS OUTPUT BECOME A "CENTRAL LINK" IN THE SYSTEM OF TARGETS?

Our major planning target, and thus statistical target, is the "gross output." Most criticisms against this target are concerned with multiple counting as a product passes through several stages of manufacturing. In fact, this is not the major weakness of the target. Insofar as one enterprise is concerned, a product is generally counted only once. Therefore, the "gross output" reflects the true output without multiple counting. In the whole national economy, multiple counting of "gross output" merely reflects the connections among various production departments (especially the connections between the producer goods department and the consumer goods department) and turnover in the whole society. The national economic balance tables reflect these connections and turnover exactly through these multiple countings. However, the relative weights of the various departments in the national economy should, of course, be computed by the "net output," and not the "gross output." This is so because the measurement of relative contributions by the various economic departments is not part of the responsibility of the "gross output."

The biggest weakness of the "gross output" target lies in its inability to adjust to enterprise management, i.e., production needs. This is because "gross output" includes both newly created value and transferred value. Newly created value refers to value created by the expended labor of the staff and workers of each enterprise. Transferred value refers to the value of materials and the depreciation of fixed assets. It is value created by the staff and workers of other enterprises. The relative weights of these two components relate primarily to the relative weights of materials and labor. And they differ among various production departments or among different products produced in one production department or enterprise. But what is important for assessing the production performance of enterprises is not the transferred value, not the amount of materials used, but the value newly created by labor. Production development does not refer to the increase of transferred value, but to the increase of newly created value. We can illustrate this point by several examples.

Example 1: A farmer harvests 10 dou of food grain with one dou of seeds in the first year. In the second year, he enlarges his cultivated area and plants 2 dou of seeds. But he harvests only 11 dou of food grain. If the "gross output" target is used, then there is a 10 percent increase in the second year compared with the first year; even though the net harvest is 9 dou in both years if the seeds are deducted. In other words, the farmer's wealth in the second year does not exceed that of the first year. Moreover, there is an increase of fertilizers and labor used in the second year. Therefore, his net income or net output in the second year must be less than that of the first year. Worse still, even if his second year's harvest was only 10.5 dou, his "gross output" target still shows a 5 percent increase. In fact, if the seeds are deducted, his second year's harvest amounts to only 8.5 dou, a 5.5 percent decrease from the first year. (If other costs were deducted, the decrease in output is even more.)

Example 2: A farm machine plant produces double-wheeled double-share plows in the first half of the year. Because this product requires a lot of materials but very little labor, two-thirds of the annual production assignment is easily completed. In the second half of the year, the plant manufactures agitating harvesters. This product requires a lot of labor and very little material. Consequently, although the staff and workers put a lot of effort into production and technical improvement, only one-third of the annual assignment is completed. According to the "gross output" target, the plant should be rewarded in the first half of the year and punished in the second half of the year. But the leadership thinks that the first half year's performance is not that good, and the second half year's performance is not all that bad.

Example 3: A plant that produces measurement and cutting instruments often produces several thousand different kinds of products according to the needs of its customers. In general, measurement instruments require little material and a lot of labor to make, and cutting instruments require little labor and a lot of materials. For example, 64.3 percent of the cost in producing a measurement instrument called the slip gauge consists of labor, only 35.7 percent consists of materials. In another measurement instrument called the dial gauge, 69.3 percent of its cost consists of labor, only 30.7 percent consists of materials. Also, the accuracy requirements of these precision instruments are very high. The errors cannot exceed a tiny fraction of the width of the human hair. They must therefore be produced by highly skilled labor. However, the case is different for cutting instruments. The labor cost of a kind of triple-blade milling cutter represents only 5.9 percent of the total cost. The other 94.1 percent represents material cost. Therefore, if the plant received orders mostly for precision measurement instruments, it would be quite difficult for it to fulfill its gross output target. In order to balance its product mix, it must produce some cutting instruments, regardless of the amount of orders received. As a result, there is often an unwanted inventory accumulation in the warehouse. In the first half of 1956, among the 8.84 million yuan of inventory in measurement and cutting instruments of the First Machine-Building Ministry, 7.61 million yuan consisted of cutting instruments. But, on the other hand, many precision measurement instruments were in short supply.

From the above examples, we can see that because the "gross output" target does not distinguish between newly created value and transferred value, namely it confuses labor and material components, it cannot accurately reflect the actual production conditions of the enterprise. Therefore, it cannot be used to assess enterprise performance.

The "gross output" target cannot correctly reflect enterprise size, i.e., its scale of production, either. Suppose there are two yarn spinning plants with equal number of spindles and labor employment. But one spins 80-count fine yarn, and the other 16-count coarse yarn. Therefore, the amount of materials used in the latter is seven times that of the former and the "gross output" is more than 2.5 times.

The "gross output" target often does not encourage the producers to save materials or to substitute cheaper ones for more expensive ones. On the contrary, it encourages them to produce more products that use expensive materials and to use expensive materials or inappropriate materials on ordinary products. Machine-building plants are only too eager to use copper and avoid iron as materials. But we all know that the task of modern industrial technology lies in knowing how to find substitutes for expensive materials, such as copper, and not to substitute copper for iron. Therefore, the "gross output" target does not and cannot motivate enterprises to produce light weight, inexpensive products of good value. Instead, it can only motivate them to make heavy and expensive products.

CONSTANT PRICES

Our present "gross output" target is computed at constant prices. But all financial accounts in the enterprise are recorded at current prices. This method divorces "gross output" from reality. In the financial account, the unit price of a product may be 4 yuan. But the constant price may be 5 yuan. The unit price of another product may be 10 yuan in the financial account, but only 9 yuan at constant prices. The difference between constant price "gross output" and current price "gross output" is often substantial. In some plants and bureaus, the difference may be as great as one to two times, or even more. It is not possible to manage enterprise finance by relying on this unrealistic account. Then, why do we compute this false account? The reason is that constant price "gross output" is computed for formulating national economic plans. It measures the growth rate of output from various departments. The purpose of developing the national economy is to increase social material wealth. But material wealth is use value which cannot be easily compared or aggregated. Therefore, it is still necessary to use money as the common yardstick. However, fluctuating prices must be fixed at some level in order to observe the growth rate of material wealth in physical terms.[1]

Therefore, we have two accounts. One is the major account. This is used for policy making, formulating national economic plans, observing the relative positions of various departments, and studying time series. This account emphasizes the use value of physical production and changes in physical quantities. This is the account of constant price "gross output" used for planning and statistics.

Another account is the subsidiary account computed at current prices. It is indispensable for enterprise financial management (namely economic accounting) regarding capital fund, costs, profit, and wages.

We keep both accounts. The leadership often appeals to the enterprise management personnel to attain comprehensive fulfillment of targets. That is to say, not only must the gross output target be fulfilled, the financial, quantity and quality targets, etc., must also be fulfilled. But the enterprise management personnel often pay little attention to the financial account and concentrate their attention on the "gross output" targets. This is because the profit quota to be sent to the higher level, called planned profit, is fixed. Regardless of the financial conditions of the enterprise, this amount is automatically deducted from its account by the bank. The wage standard cannot be changed either. And it is not easy to lower costs. Therefore, the key to solving enterprise financial problems lies in the circulating capital quota and bank credit. But these are all tied to the "gross output." Only when the "gross output" target is fulfilled will all the problems be solved. If the "gross output" target is not fulfilled, even though the newly created net output is increased, and the targets for cost and profit are fulfilled, the state plan is still regarded as unfulfilled. Moreover, the enterprise will face financial problems owing to shortage of circulating capital and bank credit. This is why most people emphasize the fulfillment of the "gross output" target and many illusions and fake reports are created. For example, in the machine-building industry, once a prototype is made, the materials shipped to the workshop can be counted into the "gross output" as "product in process." Before the privately owned plants were transformed, some (state) enterprises farmed out some of their planned work assignments to the private plants and put only finishing touches on the products when they were returned. And yet the whole products were included into their own "gross output."

All this tells us that the constant price "gross output" target is a target for the major account of the national economy. It should not be used to assess enterprise performance and to constrain or replace the accounts for enterprise financial management.

But how to make these two accounts (planning and statistical targets and financial accounts) complementary? It is, of course, possible to make more detailed product quantity and quality targets to plug loopholes in the "gross output" target. But this is a blind alley that leads nowhere.

Product quantity is admittedly a very important planning target. Without this target, it is not possible to compute material balance for the national economy. And without material balance, there is no such thing as national economic planning. Therefore, this target is indispensable for national planning, as well as enterprise planning. Although the capitalist produces only for profit, no plant owner or trust manager ever forgets how much and what varieties of product should be produced. The purpose of national economic development is to increase material wealth directly. Therefore, it is all the more important that we pay attention to product variety and quantity.

Obviously, the problem does not lie in whether the product quantity target at a certain level should be dispensed with. Rather, it lies in how these targets are to be formulated. For example, the Second Five-Year Plan required that we produced 12 million tons of steel in 1962. Who can say such a target is not important? Nobody, of course. On the contrary, this is one of the most important targets in China's industrialization program.

Therefore, product quantity targets are necessary at the State Planning Commission, the State Economic Commission, the Ministry of Metallurgy, and various iron and steel companies. But iron and steel products are of many varieties. Can all these varieties be specified by central planning agencies and in the ministry plans? Obviously not. Past criticisms against too much and too rigid targets relate to these targets. These targets should be decentralized and managed at different levels. Therefore, these product quantity targets at the central planning agencies can only be very general. Concrete varieties should be determined in the annual enterprise plans. Even annual enterprise plans should be adjusted to suit consumer needs and concrete conditions. One planning worker once asked an enterprise leader how to improve planning work. The latter replied that unanticipated tasks (referring to customer orders) often disrupted the fulfillment of plans. In my view, if this enterprise leader was truthful in what he said, his reply simply reflected his subjective bureaucratic attitude toward management because he seemed to think that it was more important to stick to subjectively determined plans than to cater to objectively determined requirements. Otherwise, his reply was merely obtuse sarcasm about planning.

Since product quantity targets should be managed at different levels, since their determination should not be rigid and must be adjusted to suit objective requirements, and since the same quantity of different product variety often requires different materials and labor with consequently substantially different values, they are not suitable comprehensive targets for motivating enterprise management. And however important they are as our goals in developing the national economy, they cannot be leading central targets.

WHERE SHOULD WE START IMPROVING PLANNING AND STATISTICAL METHODS?

How, then, should we improve our planning and statistical methods? We will not be concerned with all the targets and methods here. We will be concerned with only: (1) what central targets should be controlled in planning and statistics and how these targets should be computed; and (2) some questions relating to the planning system and financial policy in improving planning and statistical methods.

The following four basic principles should be followed to improve present planning and statistical methods: (1) the basic targets in planning and statistics should be those that can advance enterprise management and not restrict it; (2) planning and statistical targets should be coordinated with financial accounts used for financial management. These two accounts should not be allowed to impose restrictions on one another; (3) planning and statistical targets should not overemphasize physical quantity, i.e., use value. They should also pay attention to labor consumption, i.e., value. The latter should be given more attention at lower levels; and (4) so-called central targets should be central links in enterprise management. Their fulfillment should facilitate the fulfillment of other targets.

As was mentioned in the first section, our present "gross output" target does not meet these above-mentioned principles. Although product quantity targets are very important, they cannot be leading comprehensive targets that can be usefully controlled from the top to the bottom. In the Soviet Union, it has been suggested for a long time that "gross output" be replaced with "net output," or that the latter be used to supplement the former. The "value added" target used in Russia's garment industry is an attempt to abandon "gross output" in favor of "net output." ("Value added" is gross of capital depreciation to facilitate computation.)

But why was the "net output" target not adopted in the past? Why is the "value added" target used only in the garment industry in the Soviet Union? This is because there are technical problems in computing constant price "net output." "Net output" is obtained by deducting material consumption from "gross output." It is possible to calculate the materials consumed and the current price for each product from accounting records. But it is almost impossible to require an enterprise to compute the constant prices of all the thousands of new materials, spare parts, and components used for each product.

But, as was mentioned above, constant prices are used to formulate and examine long-term plans, to facilitate comparison among yearly figures over time, and to compute the major accounts of various departments of the national economy. They are not very useful for enterprise management. We must therefore ask why constant prices should be used to formulate and evaluate annual plans and to formulate and evaluate enterprise plans. If annual enterprise plans are formulated and evaluated at current prices, constant price figures used for five-year plans can still be obtained from the current price figures in annual enterprise plans through deflating. This way, net output and profit figures can be directly obtained from enterprise financial accounts. These can then be used as basic targets in planning and statistics. Thus the targets that need to be controlled in planning and statistics are also the ones that need to be controlled in enterprise management. Not only will enterprise economic accounting be facilitated, the two sets of accounts can also be consolidated into one to conserve effort.

Some people think that there are only technical problems, and no problems of principle, in using net output for planning. But they think that these problems of principle are involved when profit is used as a basic planning target.

In fact, for our present purpose (to formulate and evaluate enterprise production plans), there is no difference in principle between net output and profit. The latter is even "netter" than the former when wages are deducted. (Net output is equivalent to v + m in Marx's formula. Profit is only a part of m.)[2] Therefore, profit is the most concentrated manifestation of enterprise performance. In this case, the "profit" target is even better than the "net output" target. We should not be afraid to use the "profit" target simply because only the capitalists produce for profit and the socialist society produces for material wealth. Although the purpose of socialist production is fundamentally different from capitalist production, we should not avoid methods which can facilitate enterprise economic accounting simply because the capitalists have used them.

But if profit becomes a central target, will enterprise managers' capitalistic pursuit of profit for their own enterprises at the expense of national interests lead to market confusion?

Basically not. This is because, first, the use of profit as a central target in planning and statistics does not eliminate other targets, such as product quantity and quality (but product quantity targets should be managed at various levels). Second, single-minded capitalistic pursuit of profit is possible only when prices are not rational and market is not controlled. If prices are rational and are adjusted periodically, and if the market is well managed, then there will be no loopholes to exploit. If we could stabilize the market and eliminate speculation and manipulation even when there were large numbers of private industrial and commercial enterprises, should it be more difficult to control a smaller number of state enterprise cadres who are well organized and well led?

The greatest advantage of the "profit" target is that it reflects the annual production conditions and it can promote enterprise management. The fulfillment of this target not only will not hinder the fulfillment of other targets, but its fulfillment will automatically facilitate the fulfillment of other targets. To fulfill the net output target and the profit target, it is necessary to fulfill the product quantity target, and to pay attention to costs and labor productivity. Therefore, although "profit" itself is only a value target, material wealth will increase with the increase in profit and net output.

If "profit" is to be used as a central target in planning and statistics, the following questions relating to economic policies and financial systems should be considered by comrades in theoretical research and practical work so that this target can be accurately calculated, economic accounting can be truly enforced in enterprises and the national economy, and financial management can be strengthened.

The first problem relates to price policy. In the past, because the role played by the law of value in the socialist economy was theoretically denied or underestimated, prices were determined according to policy and not to value. More exactly, value was considered only within the context of policy or at most within the context of cost. For example, prices of consumer goods were not to be set so high as to enlarge the price differential [between agricultural goods and industrial goods], lest the worker-peasant alliance and the living standards of the staff and workers be adversely affected. Prices of producer goods, especially allocation prices applicable to state enterprises, were to be set as low as possible. Only material cost needed to be covered. In other words, prices and value were considered primarily from the viewpoints of circulation and the distribution and redistribution of national income. The need for economic accounting in the production process itself was seldom considered. These viewpoints led to the belief that only light industry was responsible for accumulation. Heavy industry was not responsible for accumulation. In China, the continual existence until recently of a large number of private industrial and commercial enterprises somewhat limits the development of this one-sided subjective price policy. But, if we continue to pay little attention in theory or in principle to this problem, it will continue to develop in this direction. For example, prices for heavy industrial products are not currently high compared with those for light industrial products, because as far as the capital profit rate is concerned, it is much lower than that for light industry. But there have long been calls for price reduction in heavy industrial products. If the prices of heavy industrial products were lower than their value, economic accounting would be adversely affected. Expensive producer goods would be used as if they were cheaper, leading to waste in production. This is no good for the national economy. In fact, prices that are too high or too low disrupt the proportional relationships and economic accounting in the national economy. Therefore, a correct price policy should be based on value. Profit (capital profit rate, not cost profit rate) in light and heavy industries should be more or less the same. State accumulation could be obtained more in the form of taxes and taxes need not be confined to light industrial products. A stricter separation between taxes and profit is beneficial to economic accounting.

The second problem relates to the accounting of fixed capital assets. This is not only the problem of statistical workers, but also the problem of planning workers, financial workers, and enterprise leaders. At present, the estimation of fixed assets in our enterprises is very chaotic. On this basis, accurate cost accounting is all but impossible. Taking inventory and reestimating the value of fixed assets is a very complicated and resource consuming job. In the past, most people favored or objected to this job primarily from the financial viewpoint. In fact, it is more important to look at the problem from the viewpoint of enterprise economic accounting.

Another manifestation of the neglect of fixed asset accounting is the opposition to capital profit in favor of cost profit.[a] It is wrong to say that capital profit is a capitalist concept. This is not only a question of capital, but also a question of labor. This is because those fixed assets which fully participate in the production process of material wealth are themselves embodied labor. It is not without reason that more embodied labor (fixed assets) needs to be

a) For a detailed discussion of the differences between capital profit and cost profit, see Chapter 6 in this volume, pp. 128–29. — K.K.F.

accumulated in heavy industrial departments than in light industrial departments before people can expand their live labor. The reason is that live labor can then be more productive and more material wealth can be created as a result. If the labor productivity of workers in heavy industry with higher organic composition of capital is not higher than that of workers in light industry, then it does not pay society first to embody part of its labor before using live labor. The capital investment is no longer necessary. If we do not properly calculate the value of existing capital assets, it follows that we will neglect the calculation and analysis of new fixed assets and their investment returns. For example, we know that the cost of power generation in hydroelectric power plants is lower, and often much lower, than that in thermal power plants. For this reason alone, we would prefer to build hydroelectric power plants rather than thermal power plants. We also know that the production cost in large plants is always lower than that in small plants. This is why many people prefer to build large rather than small plants. But this is only because we calculate only cost profit and not capital profit. If, in addition to cost calculation, we also calculate investment returns, capital availability, and length of construction time, then the conclusion would be very different.

Third, to calculate accurately commodity value and do a good job in economic accounting, it is necessary to have a correct depreciation policy. The average depreciation rate of fixed assets in the various departments of our national economy was 1.4 percent in 1952, 2.4 percent in 1953, 2.4 percent in 1954, and 2.8 percent in 1955. In other words, the period ranges from thirty-five years to more than seventy-one years. The average depreciation rate of fixed assets in industry was 3.4 percent in 1955, and the depreciation period was about thirty years. In transportation, the depreciation rate was 1.6 percent in 1955, and the depreciation period was about sixty years. In other words, our depreciation considers only physical depreciation and not invisible depreciation. Annual depreciation is then obtained by dividing the value of a fixed asset by the number of years that it can physically function. This is then added onto the value of the product. But first, the price of a machine is always higher when it is first produced. And with the improvement of production technology and mass production, its price then gradually decreases. In thirty to sixty years, its price must fall a great deal. Second, because of the invention and production of new machines serving similar purposes, existing old machines often suffer a substantial drop in value and may even be retired completely because of obsolescence (low productivity and higher cost). Therefore, before a machine has been physically worn out, its value may have been reduced for the two reasons above. This value reduction is called invisible depreciation. The faster the technological improvement, the faster is this process of invisible depreciation.

The capitalist dreads technological backwardness. To avoid loss owing to invisible depreciation of fixed assets, he raises his depreciation rate. During the Second World War, the depreciation period in the United States was set at five years. In 1954, the "declining balance method" was announced. This method allows a higher depreciation rate in the beginning of the depreciation period. The rate decreases gradually in later years. For example, the first year may be 40 percent, the second year 24 percent. In other words, 64 percent of the asset value is recouped in the first two years. The depreciation rate in the last three years is 14 percent, 8 percent, and 5 percent, respectively.[3] Of course, another reason for such high depreciation rates is that the capitalist can conceal his profit to evade income tax. But it is difficult to say that this is the major reason. The major reason is that he fears the loss from value depreciation of his fixed assets owing to the rapid advance of modern technology.

In the past, invisible depreciation was not taken into account in socialist countries. This concept was even denied in theory on account of its capitalist connotation. But this position has been criticized since 1955. The neglect of invisible depreciation has been found to be unsound in theory and detrimental in practice. The major problem is that it hinders the renovation of facilities and technological improvement.

Under the same influence which denies the existence of invisible depreciation, there is another extremely harmful practice. This is the definition of major repair. According to the current system, major repairs cannot involve changing the appearance and basic functions of existing equipment. If this scope is exceeded, they are no longer considered as major repairs but "renovation" or "capital construction" instead. They must then be approved by another procedure. We all know that investment in capital construction is tightly controlled so as to guarantee key projects. Miscellaneous "renovation" or "capital construction" projects are generally not easily approved.

Consequently, examples like the following, though highly irrational, are very widespread (as they are naturally inherent in the current system).

For example, a shipyard under the Shipbuilding Bureau has since Liberation repaired several big oceangoing ships belonging to the same customer. These vessels have been in disrepair. Two of them were in such bad shape that 80 to 90 percent of their steel plates and 50 percent of their angle steel had to be replaced. The repair fees amounted to 30 to 50 percent of the expenses of building new ones. Some of them reached more than 80 percent. The labor time required to repair represented 50 to 60 percent of the time needed to build new ones. Some even required more time than building new ones. In general, these repairs are not more economical than building new ones. Because according to the definition of "major repair," all basic equipment in the ship, especially the entire engine and all the other machinery, had to be repaired to restore the original appearance and functions. Therefore, even if all the moving parts of a machine have been changed, the nonmoving parts (shells) still remain the same. As a result, these ships are very inefficient, with a maximum speed of only 10 knots. In the present commercial fleet of Japan, the lowest speed is 16 knots. Ships with such low efficiency as ours would have been sold as scrap long ago in Japan. The engineers and workers in the shipyard were amazed every time when this customer insisted on spending so much to buy a new antique ship. But the customer had to contend with restrictions imposed by the financial system.

When invisible depreciation is ignored in economics, and technological improvements are forbidden in major repairs under our present financial system, old plants built several decades ago can coexist with new plants equipped with the world's most advanced technology. Therefore, the average productivity of the whole department can be only one-half to one-third that of the highest labor productivity in the most advanced plant. (For example, if as we have pointed out the depreciation period of industrial fixed assets was about thirty years, and the depreciation period of transportation equipment about sixty years in 1955, then it follows that industrial equipment purchased in the Northern Warlord period, and cars and boats left over from the Qing dynasty and the end of the nineteenth century can still be used today with no technological improvement. Is this conceivable?)

This curious but harmful theory and practice have their historical origin. This theoretical tendency of ignoring or downplaying investment returns and invisible depreciation is in keeping with the theoretical denial of the law of value (which admits only the use value but not the value of material wealth). Practically speaking, care and maintenance of all equipment had to be emphasized at the beginning of socialist construction, especially in the recovery period when technology was backward and finance was tight. Even backward and old equipment is better than no equipment. Therefore, appropriations were provided for major repairs. After a number of years, the major repair expenses added up to more than the cost of a modern machine. But when all the parts of the old machine had been replaced, their efficiency (productivity) was still extremely low. These "renewed old machines" end up wasting more fuel, raw material, and labor. In other words, what starts out as a means to save labor and materials ends up wasting both. To avoid this bind, we must calculate investment returns constantly (including capital construction and major repairs).

When we suggest that invisible depreciation should be taken into account and that the depreciation rate should be raised, we are not suggesting that equipment should be quickly depreciated and thrown away indiscriminately. What we are saying is that we must do some calculation. Should they be used the same way as before, or should they be used with some technological renovation, or should they be melted down as scrap? We must calculate not only whether live labor would be saved but also whether embodied labor would be saved. When more is spent in technological renovation of old equipment, key construction projects would be adversely affected. Here we must also consider whether new construction is always better than renovation. In general, renovation saves labor and money and produces faster returns. If this is the case, we must emphasize renovation more. The problem is that when we are dealing with a big renovation project such as that involving the Anshan Steel Company, the profitability can be determined by the Central authority and the State Planning Commission. But when we are deciding whether a thicker pipe should be installed in a particular furnace, or whether another motor should be installed on a particular lathe, or such similarly sundry projects, the Central authority cannot be relied on to solve the problem. Instead, power should be delegated to the enterprise, or the masses should be mobilized to solve the problem. Therefore, the financial system should allow the enterprise to keep more money and to relax the definition of major repairs.

In sum, the most fundamental point is still the problem of promoting growth in social labor productivity by calculating the amount of socially necessary labor. This is a theoretical problem, a policy problem, and a system problem. It is also an important problem that every statistical worker must concern himself with in his own post.

Tongji gongzuo jianbao [Statistical Work Bulletin], 1956, No. 29.
Tongji gongzuo [Statistical Work], 1957, No. 13.

NOTES

1. Increase in material wealth is an increase in use value and not in value. In a relatively short period of time (for example, in one five-year plan period), there is not much increase in the labor force in the whole national economy. Therefore, there is not much increase in value added (value equals labor time). Economic development and increase in labor productivity are reflected in more material wealth created by the same amount of labor. Or an equal amount of material wealth can be created with less labor. In other words, its value is less. Therefore, value targets cannot directly reflect production development, only quantity targets can reflect production development. This is all very clear in theory. But in practice, when the "gross output" target is used, one's perception is confused and it is often treated as a value target.

2. m also includes taxes. But taxes need not arise from one department alone. Some part, or even a greater part, of them are contributed by other economic departments but are merely realized in this department. They should not be included. But profit, under reasonable prices, is basically produced by one department. The problem of prices is discussed below.

3. An-dong-nuo-fu, Capital Depreciation in the United States After the Second World War, in Jingji yicong [Translation Series on Economics], 1956, No. 8, p. 54.

3

The Role of "Value"

What is value? What is the law of value? The number of papers and monographs written on these two topics by our economists in the ten years since Liberation alone totals more than several million words. There are, of course, many excellent interpretations. But many are "mere conceptual disputes that barely touch on the essence of the problem." Not only are noneconomists not interested in these disputes, even economists are bored with them. Comrade Xue Muqiao's suggestion that we should "avoid getting involved in conceptual disputes"[1] makes exactly this point.

But even here there are contradictions. There are, of course, many papers on "value" and "law of value." There is, however, no standard interpretation of these two concepts among economists. Also, we can see below that the interpretation of these two concepts changes even in the same paper by the same author. Obviously, it is absolutely necessary that this conceptual confusion among economists with respect to these basic concepts in political economy be cleared up. More importantly, this conceptual confusion brings about great harm to practice. For example, we can see from many incidents in the process of forming people's communes and the Great Leap Forward in the past year that because of some people's misinterpretation of the two very important concepts of commodity and value (they were treated as purely capitalist concepts), commodity production was suppressed, and the nature of collective ownership in the commune was briefly ignored.

Although there are already too many papers on concepts, the concepts are still not clearly explained. Thus more discussion is needed. We cannot simply "avoid getting involved in conceptual disputes." Furthermore, there is a lack of consensus among economists on many issues. Sometimes, what A considers as empty talk is considered by B as a matter of immense theoretical importance.

Or vice versa. But there can only be one truth. Only through discussion or disputes can the truth be discovered.

There are only two alternatives: either we fail to touch on the essence of a problem because we are afraid of falling into the trap of conceptual discussion and therefore try to "avoid getting involved in conceptual disputes," or we can encourage academic discussion (including conceptual disputes). If we do the former, we can never clarify conceptual confusion. But if we do the latter, then there inevitably will be a certain amount of empty talk that is unrelated to reality. Perhaps only further discussion can solve this problem.

In his preface to A Contribution to the Critique of Political Economy, Marx said: "But at the entrance to science, as at the entrance to hell, the demand must be posted: 'Here all mistrust must be abandoned. And here must perish every craven thought.'"[a]

Marx dramatized the difficulty of theoretical research by comparing it with entering hell. But I feel that there is another sense in which this verse can be quoted, that is, theoretical research is hazardous work. If the method is wrong, we are liable to fall into the hell of unreality whereby theory is pursued for the sake of theory, concepts for the sake of concepts, and science for the sake of science. But just as Marx said, we cannot hesitate in front of the entrance to science, and we cannot let fear overcome us. We should constantly remind ourselves not to divorce ourselves from reality in our theoretical research, and not to engage in empty disputes. But we cannot stop eating simply because we sometimes choke while eating, nor can we avoid conceptual disputes. For this means that we will allow conceptual confusion to persist.

Therefore, my paper will start with defining what value is and what the law of value is. It is all but inevitable that I will engage in discussion with some comrades engaged in theoretical research.

LET US START WITH WHAT THE LAW OF VALUE IS

What is value? We will all say that value is determined by the amount of socially necessary labor. Labor is a "value-creating substance."[2] We all seem to have a uniform understanding of this point. But as soon as we talk about what the

a) Sun translated this passage in Dante's Divine Comedy from the Russian edition. English translation based on the English edition of Selected Works of Marx and Engels published by Progress Publishers, Moscow, 1969, volume 1, p. 506. — K.K.F.

law of value is, and how this law operates, we all differ in our interpretation. From our different interpretations of the law of value, we can infer that deep down there is really no uniform understanding of the concept of value among us. In theoretical work and academic research, we cannot seek a common ground while reserving differences. Rather, we must seek differences while preserving the common ground. If in academic research we seek a common ground while reserving differences, there will always be peace. There will be no need to do research or engage in discussion. But neither will there be any progress. (Of course, we do not dispute for the sake of dispute.) Since we do not seem to have much disagreement on the concept of value, we will put this issue aside for the moment and start with what the law of value is. Once we have clarified this point, we will return to the concept of value and see if our understanding is really that uniform.

The publication of Stalin's Economic Issues in Soviet Union's Socialism in 1953 stimulated an upsurge of research and discussion on the law of value among Chinese economists.

At that time, the period of economic recovery in China was near its end. And the First Five-Year Plan was just starting. The capitalist economy and individual peasant and handicraft economies were still widespread. It was, therefore, natural that economists related their research on the law of value to the spontaneous influence of the capitalist economy and individual economies. In the articles published by economists in newspapers and journals on the law of value, the relative weight of the capitalist economy and individual economies in the national economy always served as a point of departure and background. Some economists almost treated the law of value as belonging to the same categories as free market, the law of market, market competition, and capitalist spontaneous influence. They put the law of value in opposition to planning. Many economists thought that planning should be applied to the state economy, while the law of value should be applied to the capitalist economy and individual economies. The law of value and the law of planning were treated as competitors. At most, the former was treated as a supplement to the latter (wherever the latter's influence could not reach). Where the influence of planning could reach, the law of value did not apply. Where the influence of planning could not reach, the law of value was tolerated.

In short, the law of value was treated as an economic law for the capitalist society. The reason why the law of value was still allowed to exist in the socialist society was because capitalist economy and commodity economy still existed. Therefore, the law of value had to be restricted in the socialist society, just as capitalist economy and commodity economy had to be restricted and transformed. Therefore, right from the start when Chinese economists began to study the law of value, the emphasis was on how to restrict it. Furthermore, they regarded the restriction of the law of value and the strengthening of the state economy equally as a kind of victory in economic work at that time.[3]

In 1956, after a decisive victory was won in China's socialist transformation of its agriculture, handicraft industry, and capitalist industry and commerce, an upsurge of discussion on value and the law of value in relation to the planning system and planning methods was started among economists. Finally, a third discussion on value and the law of value was started after the Great Leap Forward in industrial and agricultural production and nationwide communalization of the rural areas last year. Economists were interested in studying the commune system and the future of commodity production after communalization. After the "Resolutions on Some Issues Relating to the People's Commune" was announced, the Party repeatedly emphasized that the law of value must be respected in developing commodity production and in exchange. From then on, our understanding of the law of value became more comprehensive.

But most economists still regarded the law of value as applicable only to commodity economy, particularly to capitalism. Comrade Yang Yingjie said in his "The Planned Economy and the Law of Value," published in Jihua jingji [Planned Economy] , 1957, No. 6: "The law of value is an economic law of commodity production and exchange." "The law of value regulates production, exchange, and other aspects through the blind market supply-demand relationship and the 'vicious circle' of capitalist 'crisis — depression — recovery — expansion.'"[4] If the law of value is by its very nature such a vicious law, then when it is necessary to use it in the socialist society we must maintain full vigilance and also restrict and control it. Comrade Guan Mengjue warned us with just such a high degree of vigilance in his paper "Some Issues Relating to Our Present Commodity Production and the Law of Value":

> ... Let us not forget that in the long past history, the law of value was associated with private ownership. Particularly under the capitalist system, it

spontaneously regulated production and circulation and became a lever for anarchic production. At present, under the socialist system, although it has turned over a new leaf and together with commodity production has been put on the basis of public ownership of the means of production, it still retains its untamed nature. If we do not pay attention to controlling it, it will exert its negative function and run rampant.[5]

This graphic depiction of the law of value by Comrade Guan Mengjue also graphically reflects a widespread conception of the law of value among economists. The characteristic of this conception is a confusion between an objective economic law which can exist independently of our subjective wishes and subjective economic policies based on it, and a confusion between an objective economic law itself and the different roles it plays under different social and historical conditions.

As an objective economic law that exists independently of our subjective wishes, the law of value carries on in its own way regardless of how people try to restrict it and whether people respect it. As to the different roles that the law of value performs under different conditions and the forms in which these roles manifest themselves, they can only be changed as social and historical conditions change. If social and historical conditions do not change, then it is futile for people to try to change its roles and the form in which these roles manifest themselves. For herein lies the objective and independent nature of the law of value. As to how our policies are to be determined, this is quite another matter. Whether we adopt revisionist policies that create conditions for capitalist spontaneous influence, or adopt subjective policies based on wishful thinking that run counter to objective economic laws, or adopt Marxist-Leninist policies to propel history forward by changing historical conditions in accordance with objective laws, can influence the directions of events. But they cannot by themselves negate the objective and independent nature of economic laws. Only through changing social and historical conditions (for example, through the socialist transformation of the capitalist economy and individual economies) can our policies influence the roles economic laws play.

As a result of the above-mentioned confusion, there are different interpretations of the concept relating to the law of value in our discussion. We refer to different contents while using the same term. The law of value as understood by many economists refers merely to the regulation of production and consumption of products through deviation of prices from values. Very often, it refers to the regulating function exercised by price fluctuations resulting from spontaneous capitalist market forces, namely their automatic regulating function. The "vicious circle" alluded to by Comrade Yang Yingjie, and the "untamed nature" and "running rampant" mentioned by Comrade Guan Mengjue refer exactly to these functions.

Whenever value or the law of value are discussed, especially when the need to emphasize the law of value is raised, some economists loudly warn against committing revisionist errors. The law of value they have in mind relates also to the "vicious circle" alluded to by Comrade Yang Yingjie and the "untamed nature" and "running rampant" mentioned by Guan Mengjue. It also refers to its spontaneous functions in the capitalist economy or at least in the individual economy and the form which these functions assume. When some economists talk about the law of value, they put it in opposition to state planning. They treat the law of value and state planning as competitors. When they talk about restraining or controlling the function of the law of value, what they have in mind are the functions this law performs under the rule of spontaneous influence. Otherwise, how can the issue of restraining and controlling arise?

But, as long as the spontaneous influence of the capitalist and individual economy exists, the law of value will inevitably manifest itself in the manner described by Comrade Yang Yingjie and Comrade Guan Mengjue and will be damaging to the socialist economy. For this is what an objective law is. Under this circumstance, it is not a question of negating, restraining, or cursing the law of value (to negate a law is equivalent to what Stalin meant by eliminating a law), but a question of how to transform the capitalist economy socialistically. On the question of socialist transformation, and on the policy of how to deal with the capitalist economy and the individual economy, it is possible to commit revisionist errors. But it is also possible to commit the error of a subjective Left tendency. All these relate to the question of how to adopt correct policies, and not to whether the law of value should be negated or restrained.

What is their ultimate objective when economists talk about controlling or restraining the law of value? In fact, what they hope to achieve is stimulation or suppression of the production or sales of certain products through an active state price policy in place of the spontaneous fluctuations of market prices.

How can such an objective be achieved? In addition to socialistically transforming the capitalist economy, there must also be a correct price policy. And a correct price policy is one that observes the law of value. What does the law of value require? It requires that prices approximate rather than deviate from values. But to many economists, the law of value can only serve its stimulating and suppressing functions when prices deviate from values. Some economists think that emphasizing the law of value implies rapid price fluctuations and that prices should rapidly deviate from values. Because of this, many economists, after some pious talk about the need to respect the law of value, hasten to add that the law of value should not be overemphasized and that its importance should not be overemphasized. What they mean is that they don't want big price fluctuations. But this is a double misunderstanding. First, this is a conceptual confusion. They again confuse price policy (something subjective) with the law of value (something objective). Second, price policies should be based on objective laws, i.e., the law of value. And the law of value requires that prices approximate values and not deviate from values. This tendency for prices to approximate values in the law of value exists both in the capitalist economy and the socialist economy. Under capitalist anarchic production, the law of value regulates production automatically through exactly such a tendency. In our socialist society, we should actively make prices approximate values through calculations and planning.

In light of this, Comrade Xue Muqiao's explanation of the law of value in his "Commodity Production and the Law of Value Under the Socialist System," Honqi [Red Flag], 1959, No. 10, is much more complex than his explanations in earlier articles and the concepts of other economists. But I personally feel that his concept regarding the law of value is still not precise enough. And his explanation is still inconsistent. Comrade Xue Muqiao thinks that to influence production and sales of products through price fluctuations (i.e., higher or lower than values) is undoubtedly one function of the law of value. But another function of the law of value is to ensure that "prices of products must be based on the consumption of socially necessary labor." He thinks that these two functions are only two aspects of one function. This is where his concept of the law of value is more complete.

In this paper, Comrade Xue Muqiao emphasized that the law of value "cannot be changed by people's wishes." He compared the law of value to laws of nature and electricity. He said:

> Lightning in the sky occurs spontaneously, while electricity in an electric light is under the command of people. But if you violate the natural law of electricity, even electricity under people's control can still electrocute people and burn up buildings against people's wishes. The law of value is much like it. We can now consciously use the law of value for our benefit. This results from our observing the law of value. It does not mean that we can violate the law of value at will. It also does not mean that the law of value is no longer effective.

This is indeed well put. But, after the above paragraph, he hastened to add: "Of course, we do not favor overestimating the function of the law of value." Following this, after analyzing three different kinds of exchanges, he again warned:

> On this question about the function of the law of value, if the law of value is unlimitedly used to regulate the production and sales of consumer goods in place of state planning, as modern revisionists suggest, this is obviously a serious mistake....
>
> The state should not indiscriminately violate the principle of exchange at equal values by ignoring the function of the law of value (is it all right to do it discriminately? — this author); it also should not indiscriminately use the law of value to regulate the production and circulation of products. Nor should it rely on the law of value to regulate in place of state planning.[6]

If we can only consciously use the law of value, much like electricity and all natural laws, by actively observing it, then according to Stalin, "any violation, no matter how small, will lead to confusion and destruction of order." Therefore, there is no such thing as "indiscriminate use" or "unlimited use." What Comrade Xue Muqiao said about "indiscriminate use," "unlimited use," and "overestimating its importance" apparently do not refer to the function of the law of value or to the law of value itself. What he said about "the law of value is unlimitedly used ... in place of state planning, like what modern revisionists suggest ... " etc. apparently refers to the abandonment of control over capitalist spontaneous influence and socialist transformation of the capitalist economy and the individual economy. It is a matter of policy, a matter of political line. And it is different from the law of value. What he said about "overestimating the function of the law of value," "indiscriminate use of the law of value to regulate the production and circulation of products,... rely on the law of value to regulate in place of state planning," etc. probably refers to the policy of stimulating or suppressing production and sales through price fluctuations. Here, with the exception of the abandonment of state planning which also belongs to the above-mentioned issue of revisionist policy toward capitalist spontaneous forces, the rest are all questions of erroneous price policies. The mistake of these price policies lies not in overestimating the importance of the law of value, but in violating the requirement of this law.

Similarly, I also disagree with Comrade Xue Muqiao's position in his "Some Comments on Commodity Production and the Law of Value," Jingji yanjiu [Economic Research], No. 1, published earlier this year. He said:

> With respect to the question of whether the law of value will still play an important role in the future, I think the role of the law of value will be more restrained than in the previous period. But it will still play an important role. As long as the scope of commodity production is increasing, and not decreasing, the functions of the law of value will not be reduced to an insignificant position.
>
> After agricultural production cooperatives develop into people's communes, the influence of state planning over production in the people's communes is significantly strengthened. Many people's communes are no longer haggling over their individual interests. They courageously accept assignments from the state. In this respect, the role played by the law of value is significantly reduced. But, can we then assume that people's communes will unconditionally accept state assignments without consideration of their own interests? No! They cannot and should not do so.... Therefore, the exchange of industrial and agricultural products between the state and the communes should generally follow the principle of exchange at equal values. That is to say, the law of value still plays an important role.[7]

Here, Comrade Xue Muqiao still put the law of value in opposition to state planning. "The influence of state planning over production in the people's communes is significantly strengthened,... the role played by the law of value is significantly reduced." If one is strengthened, the other must be reduced correspondingly.

But immediately following the above paragraph, Comrade Muqiao added the following:

> Then, who regulates the production of the people's communes? Unquestionably, it is basically regulated by the state. With respect to important agricultural products, the state regulates, on the one hand, through planning,

> things like sown acreages and output quotas for food and cotton; on the other hand, it also regulates, through supply and marketing relationships, things like advance contracts and price policy. When regulation is effected through supply and marketing relationships, the law of value is also used. With respect to secondary agricultural products and sideline products, the state regulates through supply and marketing relationships. Here the law of value performs an even greater role. In the latter circumstance, the state should still be regarded as the main entity in regulating production, or the state should be regarded as playing a decisive role. The law of value is merely a tool employed by the state. Here the role of the state should not be undervalued; nor should the role of the law of value be ignored. To think that the law of value does not play a role because we admit that the state plays a decisive role or to think that we must undervalue the role the state plays simply because we admit that the law of value still plays a role both represent incomplete understanding.[8]

In this paragraph, Comrade Muqiao adopted a unified view of the role of the law of value and the role of the state (i.e., the role of state planning). They are no longer competitors. Then why, in the previous paragraph, did Comrade Muqiao say that the role of state planning "is significantly increased" and that the role of the law of value "is significantly reduced"?

Second, on the one hand, Comrade Muqiao admitted that the scope of commodity production is still increasing, and "the exchange of industrial and agricultural products between the state and communes should generally follow the principle of exchange at equal values. That is to say, the law of value still plays an important role." On the other hand, he also thought that "the role of the law of value will be more restricted than in the previous period." Then what are the functions that are to be restrained? And what are the functions that are still important? Isn't this a little unclear? This lack of clarity results from the lack of clarity in Comrade Muqiao's and other economists' concept of the law of value. Comrade Muqiao also confuses an objective economic law with the different functions this law performs, and the form in which these functions are performed under different social and historical conditions. Therefore, it is difficult to conclude from Comrade Muqiao's paper (and other papers with similar positions by other economists) what the law of value really is. Should it be respected like all objective laws? Or should we keep at a respectable distance from it?

Here, we must again go back to the conceptual dispute mentioned at the beginning of this paper. In principle, I agree with Comrade

Muqiao that we should "avoid unnecessary disputes"[9] and avoid "mere conceptual disputes that do not touch upon the essence of the issue." [10] That is to say, we must try our best not to engage in empty talk and semantic disputes. But I do not think that we should in general "avoid getting involved in conceptual disputes." Economists in China have discussed value and the law of value in the socialist society for six years or so. Still their concepts of value and the law of value are very confused. This confusion leads people in general to associate closely the "ghost" of capitalist spontaneous forces with such concepts as "value" and "law of value." Therefore, while the broad masses are all studying political economy, economists have the primary responsibility to help them separate this capitalist "ghost" from the concepts of "value" and "law of value." Even as most economists now think that "value" and "law of value" are concepts belonging to the commodity economy, we must still affirm that if commodity production and all its categories serve capitalism in a society under bourgeois dictatorship, then commodity economy and all its categories serve socialism in a socialist society under proletarian dictatorship.

What is the law of value? As the name implies, it must be a law governing the existence and operation of value as an objective category. And value, as it is commonly defined, is determined by socially necessary labor which "creates the substance of value." Then the law of value must be a law governing the existence and operation of socially necessary labor which "creates the substance of value." But most economists object to this interpretation. Economists admit that socially necessary labor creates and <u>determines</u> the <u>substance</u> of value, but they do not accept that the law governing value is the law governing the substance of value because "socially necessary labor and value are basically two different things."[11] If the law of value is not a law governing the substance of value, then logically speaking it must govern the form of value! Is this somewhat strange? Therefore, in order to further clarify what the law of value is, we must first clarify what "value" is.

WHAT IS VALUE?

What is value? Will the concept of "value" still exist in the communist society? These two questions must be studied together. Some comrades may think that this is another roundabout and impractical approach. If we cannot clarify value and the law of value in our present socialist society, how can we clarify what value and the law of value will be like in the future and unknown communist society? On the contrary, only by clarifying whether there is a value category in the communist society can we clarify the positions of value and its law in the socialist society. We can explain this position from two aspects.

First, the socialist society is not an independent societal form in the history of human development. It is a transition between the capitalist society and the communist society. In the socialist society, there exist, on the one hand, birthmarks carried forth from the womb of old society — there are many birthmarks of this kind, but they will gradually fade away; on the other hand, there arise in the socialist society many new seedlings of the communist society — these seedlings may be very small, but they are growing stronger day by day. If we look at these things merely as they appear to us now, it is often difficult to tell the difference between old and new and appreciate their essence. So the saying goes: "I don't know the real appearance of the Lu Mountains; all I know is that I am in them."

Marx told us that in order to study natural phenomena, it is necessary to use a laboratory to isolate the research objects from their original environment, and to study social phenomena it is necessary to use abstraction to strip away superficial phenomena that have nothing to do with the essence. In studying value and the law of value in our present transitional stage of the socialist society, we should also adopt such an approach. Therefore, we must observe value and the law of value in the socialist society from the viewpoint of a purely capitalist economy and from the viewpoint of a purely communist economy. Only by doing this can we clearly understand the actual content of these categories in the socialist society. But it is easier to just treat value and the law of value as capitalist economic categories, as most economists are doing now. This is so not only because the classical writers in Marxism have thoroughly analyzed the law of value in the capitalist economy, but also because our generation has actually lived through it. But it is more difficult to observe this problem from the viewpoint of the communist society because the classical writers in Marxism made very few predictions in this respect. And we do not have any actual experience with it. However, it is very important to observe from this viewpoint because we are heading in that direction.

Second, there is still another more practical reason for looking at the law of value from the viewpoint of the communist society.

Namely, to explain the internal laws governing whole people ownership. No one can deny that the whole people ownership economy (i.e., our state economy) occupies a leading position in the socialist economy. It represents the future of our communist society. Therefore, we must ask what economic laws replace the law of value which once governed here in the whole people ownership economy.

To this question, we get only one clear-cut but rather general answer: it is the law of planned and proportional development that integrally governs the national economy. There is no question about it! But those comrades who answer this way often do not realize that the plans and proportions they talk about are, if divorced from value, merely material plans and proportions (including the gross output plan at constant prices).[12] And a proportional relationship in material terms, for example the proportional relationship between number of tons of standard coal and number of kilowatts of electricity, belongs more properly to the research scope of technology science than that of the economic science. For these are all physical and chemical proportions. Confused by the gross output targets expressed at constant prices, our economists and economic workers often forget that "economics" comprises the combination of material proportions and value proportions (namely socially necessary labor). (More on this later.) In the Great Leap Forward of last year, many economic workers realized through their practice that all proportional relationships could ultimately be reduced to proportional relationships of labor power or labor. But our economic theorists have paid little attention to the question of how the value category plays its role in planning work, particularly in the internal relationships of the whole people ownership economy.

On the contrary, economists still treat "value" as a category left over from capitalism and commodity economy and have tried very hard to kick it out of the sacred ground of internal relationships in the whole people ownership economy.

In the past two or three years, the door to this sacred ground seems to have opened a little more. Many economists say: First, there still exist different ownership systems in the socialist society, and there must be commodity exchanges among these ownership systems. Second, the communist consciousness of the staff and workers in state enterprises is still not high enough in the socialist stage to dispense with material incentives. Therefore, the law of value must still play a part within the whole people ownership system.

We can see that in reality the law of value did not come in through the front gate to the sacred ground of whole people ownership system. Instead, it was admitted through its back door. The law of value is still needed simply because the whole people ownership system must still engage in exchanges with other ownership systems, and the communist consciousness of staff and workers is still not high enough. The law of value is not regarded as something needed in the production process of the whole people ownership system. Value is then not a category in the production process. It is only a category in the circulation process (for the sake of exchange). We can see from the following analysis that indeed the value category is used by many economists as a concept in the circulation sphere. Here we will say a few words in passing about the question of communist consciousness. In recent years, whenever new contradictions arise in economic life for which economists cannot or will not find any explanation from objective economic laws, a simple answer is often heard: This is a question of ideology! This is owing to low communist consciousness! It seems as if people's ideological commitment and communist consciousness are not progressing, but retrogressing. This is not only an underestimation of the consciousness of our comrades and masses (including ourselves), but is an entirely idealistic analysis.

One popular current idea goes like this: the reason why the law of value is still being "used" in the whole people ownership economy is because it must engage in exchange with other ownership systems and it must also do internal economic accounting because material incentives are still necessary to motivate staff and workers with low communist consciousness. This logic seems to imply that economic accounting would be unnecessary if their consciousness were improved. Therefore, in order to clarify the essence in the internal relationship of the whole people ownership economy, it is necessary for us to abstract from nonessential things. That is, we must abstract from its exchange relationship with other ownership systems and from the connection between ideological consciousness and material incentives, and observe the whole people ownership system as a complete communist society. Only by doing this can we discover whether the category of value can be completely eliminated in the own needs of the whole people ownership economy.

Here again I would like to remind everybody of one thing: the law of value even in the capitalist economy, unlike what some comrades often say, does not perform only purely negative, destructive functions, or only propel the "vicious circle." On the contrary, the historical function of the capitalist society has been to propel technological advances and the development of productive forces in the society. As to the socialist society, even those economists who insist that the law of value is a capitalist economic law do not deny that we must still "use" this law for "constructive purposes." Then we should ask: what other laws should be used to serve these "constructive purposes" as the transitional socialist society progresses?

In fact, if we are positive that value and the law of value are capitalist categories, we are admitting that no matter how important this law is at present, its importance will decline with the continual progress of the socialist society. But we can see that while on the one hand many economists continually restrain and underplay the importance of the law of value and wish for its demise, they are forced on the other hand to "delegate" new missions to it.

In the beginning, the law of value was allowed to participate in the big family of socialist economic laws as a spokesman for spontaneous market forces of the capitalist economy and the individual economy. Later on, after the capitalist economy and the individual economy had been socialistically transformed, it was thought that this law could still be brought under control to perform regulatory functions through state intervention to raise and lower prices. Moreover, its scope of regulation gradually expanded. At first, it was admitted that value could regulate only in the circulation sphere. Later, it was admitted that it could also regulate in the production sphere. It was then further admitted that the law of value was useful not only when prices were raised or lowered to adjust their deviation from values, it was also useful when prices were equal to values. In the past two or three years, economists have begun to emphasize the accounting function of the law of value. For example, the subtitle of Comrade Xue Muqiao's paper published in Hongqi, 1959, No. 10, is "Do Economic Accounting According to Value (Socially Necessary Labor)."

But as long as economists still treat "value" as a category in commodity economy, their position will become increasingly inconsistent as the scope of the application of the law of value is increased. The most obvious examples are the two papers by Comrade Wang Yanan on issues related to the law of value published in this year's Renmin ribao.[13] The contents of these two papers are basically the same. We cannot discover anything new after his "A Revisit to the Law of Value and Its Functions" (heading of section two in his second paper). His second paper expresses his ideas in greater detail and with greater impact. But they are also more inconsistent with his assessment of the future of value in the same paper. Because this paper of Comrade Wang Yanan's represents the common position of many economists in greater clarity, I would like to talk about it in greater detail.

In the first paragraph of his paper, he pointed out that some economists "regard the law of value as a capitalist specialty" and "consider its function only from a negative viewpoint. As a result, whenever people talk about the socialist planned economy, they automatically put it in opposition to the law of value." Consequently, "the law of value is allowed to perform its function only in the 20 percent or so of commodity production and circulation in the national economy that has not been included in the state plan,"... etc. After criticizing other economists' viewpoints, Comrade Wang Yanan arrived at this conclusion:

> The law of value is not antagonistic to the planned economy. It is a basic economic law of socialism and is a good helper to the planned and proportional development of the national economy. It plays its role in the service of the latter. The functions of the law of value must be seriously considered when plans are made and implemented.

In the second section ("A Revisit to the Law of Value and Its Functions") of this paper, he said: "The basic formulation of the law of value proposed by Marx was: socially necessary labor determines commodity value. In fact, the basic function of the law of value is also expressed herein." After describing how the law of value plays its part through determining the socially necessary labor, he summed it up:

> Therefore, this form of the law of value implies the demarcation between the advanced and the backward. In our current parlance, it is an objective social enforcer in the struggle to be the advanced and catch up with the advanced. The so-called advanced quota and advanced average quotas are realized through this form(?).

Immediately following this, he quoted a very important statement from Marx to illustrate his point: "The value of a commodity varies directly as the quantity, and inversely as the productiveness, of the labor incorporated in it."[14]

In this section he also said:

> The law of value is a common characteristic of commodity production in all societal forms. This characteristic is expressed not in a negative way but in a positive way. Its basic function is to promote production. Only under the special conditions of capitalist commodity production does it lead to serious negative effects while promoting production.

In the third section, Comrade Wang Yanan used real life examples to describe "how the law of value works in China's economic life and economic policy." In the fourth section, he appealed to everybody

> to relate the discussion of commodity production and the law of value to a correct understanding of the Party's goals and policies, and explore all effective measures that can rapidly increase social productiveness through exploiting the positive functions of the law of value.

I basically agree with these statements of Comrade Wang Yanan's, particularly those that I have underlined. I made almost the same points in an article that I wrote a little more than two years ago.[15] But having said all this, Comrade Wang Yanan arrived at the following strange conclusion at the end of his paper:

> Whether commodity production is still necessary in the highest stage of communism, and whether the law of value is still needed to promote productivity are questions that I will not attempt to answer here. If it is necessary to make a passing remark in view of the many different ideas that have been expressed on these questions, then I think commodity production is a historical form. Our present task is to promote commodity production, use the law of value to accelerate the development of our social labor productivity, and hasten the completion of the two transitions so that commodity production can be terminated and the functions of the law of value can be dispensed with.

I do not object to Comrade Wang Yanan's intention to "terminate" commodity production in the communist society, although to be precise I do not think commodity production is to be terminated by any particular people or things. Rather, it is to fade gradually away, much like the state. But after thus defining the law of value, and after providing such a perfect description of its positive functions, how can Comrade Wang Yanan then relegate the law of value to the status of a "burial object"? The definition he chose for the law of value and the functions he attributed to it are certainly not integrally related to commodity production. This conclusion of

Comrade Wang Yanan's does not seem to follow from the content of his paper. Rather it contradicts the content of his paper.

How did Comrade Wang Yanan defend his position? He did not do so at all. But other economists when faced with the same contradiction always find their way out by quoting a statement from Engels. All those who are positive that "value" no longer exists in the communist society, who think that "value" is only a category in the capitalist economy or at most in the commodity economy, base their thinking primarily on this statement. Therefore, I must ask for my reader's indulgence to allow me to quote this statement at length, so that we can understand it completely and correctly.

> From the moment when society enters into possession of the means of production and uses them in direct association for production, the labor of each individual, however varied its specifically useful character may be, is immediately and directly social labor. The quantity of social labor contained in a product has then no need to be established in a roundabout way; daily experience shows in a direct way how much of it is required on the average. Society can calculate simply how many hours of labor are contained in a steam engine, a bushel of wheat of the last harvest, or a hundred square yards of cloth of a certain quality. It could therefore never occur to it still to express the quantity of labor put into the products, which it will then know directly and in its absolute amount, in a third product. Moreover, this third product is at best relative, fluctuating, and inadequate, though formerly unavoidable for a lack of a natural, adequate, and absolute measure — time. Just as little as it would occur to chemical science still to express atomic weights in a roundabout way, relatively, by means of the hydrogen atom if it was once able to express them absolutely, in their adequate measure. Namely, in actual weight, in $1/10^{12}$th or $1/10^{24}$th of a gram. On the assumptions we made above, therefore, society will also not assign values to products. It will not express the simple fact that the hundred square yards of cloth have required for their production, let us say, a thousand hours of labor in an oblique and meaningless way, that they have the value of a thousand hours of labor. It is true that even then it will still be necessary for society to know how much labor each article of consumption requires for its production. It will have to arrange its plan of production in accordance with its means of production, which include, in particular, its labor forces. The useful effects of the various articles of consumption, compared with each other and with the quantity of labor required for their production, will in the last analysis determine the plan. People will be able to manage everything very simply, without the intervention of the famous "value." [16]

From the above quotation from Engels, it seems that the case is against retaining the concept of "value" in the communist society and the whole people ownership system proper. Comrade Wang Sihua says, "Socially necessary labor is basically not the same thing as value." He probably based his statement on this passage of Engels' quoted here. To prove that there will not be any concept of "value" in the future communist society, and to prove that the concept of "value" is still needed in today's socialist society and that the "law of value" is still important, many economists have spilled a lot of ink over this passage from Engels. It seems to be quite easy to prove that the category of "value" will no longer exist in the future communist society because Engels seemed to have said so in so many words. (In fact, he really meant "exchange value" — more of this later.) But it is a bit awkward to prove from this passage that the famous "value" is still needed now.

Economists generally try to prove that the famous value is still needed today from two aspects.

First, because at present society still does not own all the means of production and there are still two ownership systems, commodity exchange is still needed between them. Therefore, it is still necessary to emphasize the "law of value." But, as was pointed out earlier, this explanation amounts to admitting that the "law of value" only exists between the two ownership systems. So far as the internal relationships within the two ownership systems themselves, particularly within the whole people ownership system itself, are concerned, the "law of value" is dispensable.

Second, because at present society still cannot directly calculate labor, we cannot but seek help from the famous "value" in a roundabout way. Some economists explain why we cannot directly calculate labor at present in terms of technical difficulties, emphasizing the complexity of direct calculation. Some economists explain why we still cannot directly calculate labor quantity in terms of social reasons. For example, they say that there still exists the difference between complex labor and simple labor, and the difference between skilled labor and unskilled labor, etc. In fact, these are not substantive reasons. The state can now directly obtain statistical data from forms given to enterprises and communes. If only we place importance on this job, the quality and quantity of these data can be guaranteed. As to the technical difficulty of calculation, today's electronic computers can easily handle the accurate calculation of total labor consumption (including direct and indirect labor). The problem lies also in whether we attach enough importance to the calculation of socially necessary labor. Moreover, according to experts in this field, if we do not calculate by product, but only by industry (industrial sector), it is possible to calculate total labor consumption by approximation even without the help of electronic computers. As to the conversion between labor of different complexity and skill, we can use wage incomes as a conversion standard because we should admit that our wage system accords basically with the principle of distribution according to labor. Therefore, we cannot accept computational difficulty as an adequate reason (regardless of whether this difficulty is related to technical factors or social factors). This is one aspect of the issue.

More importantly, if we admit that we still cannot directly calculate labor but must use a roundabout method to express value as suggested by Engels, then we have to consider what Engels meant when he said in a roundabout way and in terms of value. Some economists think that it is only a matter of terms. That is to say, after we solve the technical problem of calculating labor in the future, we can directly say how many hours of socially necessary labor a product is worth. But at present, we must indirectly say how many units of Renminbi it is worth. If we interpret Engels' statement this way, then after the technical problem of calculation is solved, the difference between the roundabout way in terms of value and the direct way in terms of labor time is no more than an author's changing his pen names. Isn't this far too simple?

Then what is the meaning of Engels' statement, in a roundabout way in terms of value? In this passage, Engels had already made himself very clear. It means that every commodity must be expressed in terms of another commodity. That is to say, it must be expressed through an exchange relationship. How is this exchange ratio established? Does it mean that the value of each commodity can be expressed in any amount of another commodity? This is inconceivable. We all know that in a typical commodity economy, a commonly accepted exchange ratio between one commodity and another commodity or money is established only after repeated exchange. That is to say, when Engels said in a roundabout way in terms of value, or in terms of another commodity (Engels said a third product because he was talking about money), he was primarily concerned with the free market and competition. What he was talking about was, in fact, the exchange values of commodities.

Therefore, those economists who base their arguments for retaining the "value" category for the present on this passage of Engels' probably do not realize that they are in fact implicitly arguing for price determination through free market competition. We of course know that our prices are not determined in this way.

Therefore, when many economists say value they mean in fact exchange value. That is, it is market value (average price) that is established through repeated exchange (with one side of the exchange taking advantage of another). This "value" not only will not exist in the future communist society, it does not even exist in the socialist society today. Today we should encourage the method of setting prices by calculating labor cost and socially necessary labor. Whether socially necessary labor should be the objective basis of our price policy (i.e., the issue of price formation) should also be one of the topics in our research on "value" under the socialist system today.

Since the publication of my paper "Build Planning and Statistics on the Law of Value" two years ago, many comrades have criticized my contention that the "value" category would still exist in the communist society. They say that I do not understand that the concept of "value" represents a certain production relationship, i.e., it represents the commodity production relationship and the capitalist production relationship. They say that I misuse and confuse the concept. They even say that I want to build socialist planning and statistical work on the basis of a capitalist economic law, etc. In fact, I made myself very clear in that paper. When I said that we should build planning and statistics on the law of value, I did not mean the narrowly defined law of value (i.e., the law of market value). Rather, I meant the broadly defined law of value, namely socially necessary labor. But my critics object to my idea by quoting Engels' "no longer expressed in a roundabout way in terms of value." They also think that the reason "value" is still retained in today's socialist society is because it is still impossible to calculate labor directly, and it must be expressed in a roundabout way in terms of value. When they say this, they are actually confusing two different concepts, namely "value" and "exchange value." They confuse exchange value which is a roundabout expression established through free competition and repeated random exchanges (often with one side taking advantage of another) with the planned value of our socialism. In fact, it is they who are confusing the capitalist and individual production relationship with our socialist whole people ownership and collective ownership production relationship.

It is very important to distinguish between the two different concepts of "value" and "exchange value." Exchange value reflects the characteristic of the commodity production relationship in the capitalist and individual economy. And value is socially necessary labor itself embodied in product. It is not particular to the commodity economy. Political economy before Marx could not distinguish between these two concepts because economists then customarily used the concept of "value" to represent "exchange value." Marx and Engels followed the conventional usage of contemporary economists and often used "value" to represent "exchange value" for the sake of brevity (especially when they debated with the bourgeois economists who did not make a distinction between these two concepts). But in the section on "The Form of Value or Exchange Value" in the first chapter ("Commodity") of Capital, Marx explained in great detail the two different concepts of "value" and "exchange value." If we carefully examine the descriptions given to these two concepts, we can see that in many places when Marx and Engels used the term "value," it should be understood to mean "exchange value." For example, the last sentence of the quoted passage from Engels, "without the intervention of the famous 'value,'" has been only literally interpreted by many economists. They have not wondered why Engels needed to put quotation marks on "value" and qualify it with the adjective "famous." Obviously, value was here used in the conventional sense of bourgeois economics, namely, it was used to represent "exchange value."

Many economists interpret what Marx and Engels said on many occasions, that labor would no longer be expressed in terms of value after the means of production were publicly owned, to mean that the concept of "value" no longer existed in the communist society. I point out in my paper, "Build Planning and Statistics on the Law of Value" that whenever we see the phrases "in terms of" or "not in terms of" value, "value" should be read as "exchange value." If it is in terms of something, it must be referring to the form of value, namely "exchange value." Some economists think that this is also a distortion of what Marx and Engels said and based entirely on my own views. Therefore I hope my critics and readers will carefully reread the second paragraph of Section 3, "The Form of Value or Exchange Value," in Chapter 1 of Capital. In this paragraph, Marx said:

The reality of the value of commodities differs in this respect from Dame Quickly. That we don't know "where to have it." The value of commodities is the very opposite of the coarse materiality of their substance, not an atom of matter enters into its composition. Turn and examine a simple commodity, by itself, as we will, yet in so far as it remains an object of value, it seems impossible to grasp it. If, however, we bear in mind that the value of commodities has a purely social reality, and that they acquire this reality only in so far as they are expressions or embodiments of one identical social substance, viz., human labor, it follows as a matter of course, that value can only manifest itself in the social relation of commodity to commodity. In fact we started from exchange-value, or the exchange relation of commodities, in order to get at the value that was hidden behind it. We must now return to this form under which value first appeared to us.[17]

Here, Marx was very explicit. Whenever he talked about the manifestation of value, he meant "exchange value," namely "exchange relationship." For here Marx was talking about capitalist commodity value.

It is quite clear that if value must manifest itself in terms of exchange value in a commodity exchange relationship, how can value itself manifest the socially necessary labor? Therefore, we can see that whenever Marx and Engels talked about "manifest in terms of value," it should be interpreted as to mean "manifest in terms of exchange value."

In another section ("The Fetishism of Commodities and the Secret Thereof"), Marx again returned to this point:

Political economy (namely bourgeois political economy — this author) has indeed analyzed, however, incompletely, value and its magnitude, and has discovered what lies beneath these forms. But it has never once asked the question why labor is represented by the value of its product and labor time by the magnitude of that value.[18]

Here, we can see that Marx again used "represented by value" to mean "form of value," namely "exchange value." More importantly, Marx added an important footnote (No. 32 in the original edition) to the last sentence of the above paragraph. I will translate part of it as follows:

It is one of the chief failings of classical economy that it has never succeeded, by means of its analysis of commodities, and, in particular, of their value, in discovering that form under which value becomes exchange-value. Even Adam Smith and Ricardo, the best representatives of the school, treat the form of value as a thing of no importance, as having no connection with the inherent nature of commodities. The reason for this is not solely because their attention is entirely absorbed in the analysis of the magnitude of value. It lies deeper. The value-form of the product of labor is not only the most abstract, but is also the most universal form, taken by the product in bourgeois production, and stamps that production as a particular species of social production, and thereby gives it its special historical character. If then we treat this mode of production as one eternally fixed by Nature for every state of society, we necessarily overlook that which is the differentia specifica of the value-form, and consequently of the commodity-form, and of its further developments, money-form, capital-form, etc.

This quotation is a bit long. But it is very important. I hope my readers, particularly my critics, will read it carefully and repeatedly. Here Marx clearly told us: What makes bourgeois production a special and historical species of social production is the value-form, namely exchange value, and not value. Because of this, representatives of bourgeois political economy can admit that value is created by labor, objectively analyze value and the magnitude of value, but dare not look value-form in the eye. In other words, they cannot tell the difference between "value" and "exchange value." Many of our comrades insist on distinguishing capitalist production by associating "value" exclusively with it. But instead of concentrating on the substance of value, they emphasize the form of value, i.e., "exchange value." Isn't this a little odd?

For the same reason, I do not agree with the following remarks of Comrade Xue Muqiao's:

The term law of value is usually associated with commodity production. Therefore, to avoid unnecessary disputes it is better to say that state enterprises do economic accounting with the help of a value form, and not to substitute "law of value" for "value form."[19]

I do not understand why Comrade Xue Muqiao is so afraid of disputes. Admittedly, what Comrade Muqiao is talking about is unnecessary disputes. I do not favor unnecessary disputes either. But all questions boil down to what are unnecessary disputes. When Comrade Muqiao is faced with conceptual disputes, he often tries to avoid them by putting them in another way. But a new way of saying them often involves another new concept. If this new concept is inappropriate, it will lead to new disputes. To explain the concept of "value-form," Marx went to the trouble of writing a long footnote (what we have quoted is only a small part of the whole footnote) to argue with the bourgeois economists! But Comrade Muqiao wants to use "value form" to "avoid unnecessary disputes." What Comrade Muqiao means by "value form" is not the same as what Marx meant by value-form in Capital. To Comrade Muqiao, "form" simply means that value was only a "means of accounting"[20] within the whole people ownership system and in the future society. He wants to dilute the stern facade of "value" with the term "form" so as to avoid "unnecessary disputes" with those people who object to "value." But the color conveyed by the term "form" is even more intense than "value" itself, as it connotes exchange value. Here again, Comrade Muqiao is unexpectedly confronted with another dispute. The more he tries to avoid disputes, the more he gets involved with them. I hope more economists can join us in this discussion because I do not think this is an empty conceptual dispute.

To summarize what I have said, my point is: whenever Marx and Engels said that after means of production were publicly owned, individual labor would directly become social labor and need not be expressed in terms of "value" in a roundabout way, the term "value" should be interpreted as "exchange value." Other than saying "no longer be expressed in terms of value," Marx and Engels did not say that the "substance of value" would no longer exist in the future society. On the contrary, both of them said that the role of "value" in the future society would be even more important and that only in the communist society could "value" find its "proper scope of activity." In my paper, "Build Planning and Statistics on the Law of Value," I quoted the following passage from Marx to support my point:

> After the abolition of the capitalist mode of production, but still retaining social production, the determination of value continues to prevail in the sense that the regulation of labor-time and the distribution of social labor among the various production groups, ultimately the book-keeping encompassing all this, become more essential than ever.[21]

In the last two years or so, many economists have offered different interpretations of this above quotation to refute my point in that paper. Their main point is this: Marx only talked about the "determination of value," and not the "law of value." Therefore, my point is groundless. Comrade Hu Jichuang even went to the trouble of looking up all the passages in the German, Chinese, Russian, and English editions of Capital in which Marx used the concept of "value determination." He concluded:

> Therefore, value determination or the law of value determination cannot be the same as the law of value. It can be the precondition for the law of value, but

> not the law itself. For value determination seeks to answer such questions as what constitutes the value of commodities and how different value components are formed and separated. Obviously, before these questions are answered satisfactorily, we cannot begin to talk about the law of value and its functions. . . .[22]

I admire Comrade Hu Jichuang's serious attitude in scholarly research on the classical works. But I cannot agree with his viewpoint on this issue.

After quoting the above passage from Marx in that paper of mine, I said:

> Marx clearly pointed out that "the determination of value continues to prevail" in regulating labor time and distributing social labor among various production groups. Also, it would "become more essential than ever." Marx did not say the "law of value," only "the determination of value." But can this choice of terms have such pivotal importance? [23]

When I wrote that paper, I did not realize, as I do now, how narrow and fixed the interpretation which many economists have given to the "law of value" is. Therefore, I did not elaborate on this point as much as I should have. As a result, the disputes that many critics have had with me in the last two years have been conducted at cross purposes. For example, Comrade Luo Gengmo criticized as follows:

> Marx's "determination of value" cannot be referring to the law of value because commodities and the law of value will not exist then. (But I did not say that commodities and the law of commodity value would still exist either – this author.) Therefore, it was not accidental that Marx said the "determination of value," and not the law of value.[24]

Another example is Comrade Hu Jichuang's statement: The law of value

> shows how in the process of commodity production value realizes itself through deviation, and how distribution is effected among various factors of production through transformation of the income form and hence controlling production and allocating factors of production.[25]

In short, both Comrades Luo Gengmo and Hu Jichuang first defined the law of value narrowly and refused to consider or see the need to wonder whether there were other possible definitions outside their narrow confines. Then they asked rhetorically whether such a law of value could still exist in the communist society.

In the quotation from my paper, I did not realize that this law of value could only be interpreted so narrowly. To me, the important things about this quotation from Marx are: first, he affirmed that the important category and concept of "value" would still exist in the communist society; second, he pointed out that in the communist society, the "value" category "continued to prevail in the sense that the regulation of labor time and the distribution of social labor among the various production groups became more essential than ever." I did not even consider (for it was entirely unnecessary) whether "determination" and "law" were the same or different. For if Marx thought that such an important category as value would still exist in the communist society and pointed out that value would still prevail in regulating and allocating social labor, then "value" must have its law of existence and operation. As to the scope and definition of this law, I did not consider in any great detail. For this is what we have to find out and master as theoretical researchers. I really do not know what other interpretations can be given to this quotation from Marx.

In addition to the above quotation from Marx, Engels also gave us two direct instructions on this issue which we did not pay any attention to in the past.

In the past, when we read Anti-Duhring and came across the above-quoted statement "without the intervention of the famous 'value,'" we generally interpreted it to mean the rejection of the "value" category in the communist society. For we did not notice that there was a very important footnote attached to the phrase "famous 'value.'"

As long ago as 1844 I stated that the above-mentioned balancing of useful effects and expenditure of labor would be all that would be left, in a communist society, of the concept of value as it appears in political economy (Deutsch-Französische Jahrbücher). The scientific justification of this statement, however, as can be seen, was only made possible by Marx's Capital. [26]

The following is the statement Engels made in 1844 in Deutsch-Französische Jahrbücher.

Value is the relation of production costs to utility. The first application of value is the decision as to whether a thing ought to be produced at all; i.e., as to whether utility counter-balances production costs. Only then can one talk of the application of value to exchange. The production costs of two objects being equal, the deciding factor determining their comparative value will be utility.

... The contradiction between the real inherent utility of the thing and the determination of that utility, between the determination of utility and the freedom of those who exchange, cannot be superseded without superseding private property; and once this is superseded, there can no longer be any question of exchange as it exists at present. The practical application of the concept of value will then be increasingly confined to the decision about production, and that is its proper sphere.[27]

Here, Engels like Marx thought that the role of "value" was more important in the communist society. And indeed, the proper sphere for value can only be found in the communist society. For only then will value be used directly to solve problems of production and production planning, while before in the capitalist society value was primarily used to solve the exchange problem. In other words, it was used as a category in the circulation process. It affected the production process through the circulation process. But many economists now treat the influence arising from the deviation of price from value as the entire justification for the existence of "value." Isn't this analogous to the blind man who misidentified the trunk of an elephant as the whole elephant? I may sound sarcastic here, but isn't it true that the influence arising from the deviation of price from value represents a similar proportion to the whole existence and operation of value as the trunk of an elephant to the whole animal?

In summary, therefore, I think the law of value is the law governing the whole existence and operation of value. Value determination is the basis and starting point of this law. The deviation of price from value and the influence this deviation exerts is only a form which the law of value assumes in the individual economy and the capitalist economy.[28] We can regard this form of influence as basically being superseded in China today. For we no longer determine prices by the roundabout method of expressing socially necessary labor through market competition. Instead, we determine prices and make plans by directly calculating labor cost. This was exactly what I meant in 1956 when I wrote "Build Planning and Statistics on the Law of Value."

The difference between the capitalist economy and individual economy (simple commodity production), on the one hand, and the communist economy (and the internal relationship of the whole people ownership system), on the other, does not lie in the existence of the law of value in the former and the absence of the law of value in the latter. The difference lies in the fact that the law of value exerts spontaneous regulating influence in the capitalist and individual economy (simple commodity production). There, commodity value must be expressed in a roundabout way through an exchange relationship with another commodity, i.e., through exchange value. There, "these formulae (of exchange value), which bear it stamped upon them in unmistakable letters that they belong to a state of society, in which the process of production has the mastery over man, instead of being controlled by him. . . ."[29] Therefore, there the law of value not only regulates but is also the "regulator" ruling over people. But the law of value under communism and within the internal relationship of whole people ownership is controlled by people. For here "man controls the production process." And the value of products need not be expressed in a roundabout way, but can be expressed through direct calculation.

Many comrades also attempt to associate "regulating functions" with the law of value under the capitalist and individual economy so as to distinguish it from the law of value under the present socialist economy. For example, they may say that regulating functions exist only in the capitalist and individual economy but are absent in the socialist society, etc. But, from the above-quoted statement from Marx, we can see that Marx thought that in the communist society value "continued to prevail" in "regulating labor-time and distributing social labor among various production groups." Doesn't what we understand as production regulation ultimately amount to Marx's "regulating labor-time and distributing social labor among various production groups"? The earlier quotation from Engels should also be interpreted this way. The statement that "The first application of value is the decision as to whether a thing ought to be produced at all" clearly indicates production regulation. I hope my critics will not dispute on such a point as whether "determination" is the same as "law" or not. Instead, I hope they will answer the following questions. Did Marx and Engels apply the concept of "value" to the production relationship in the communist economy? Did Marx say "value continued to prevail in regulating labor-time and in distributing social labor among various production groups?" Did Engels say that in the communist society, "the practical application of the concept of value will then be increasingly confined to the decision about production, and that is its proper sphere"? And wasn't his decision about production concerned with "whether a thing ought to be produced at all"? Are not the regulation and allocation of labor and the decision whether a product should be produced at all part of production regulation?

I hope economists will not be misled by the misconception about "value" formed in the past twenty to thirty years. Instead, I hope they will carefully reexamine the several pages quoted here from Marx and Engels.

Well-meaning comrades have advised me: the purpose of your emphasis on the law of value is simply to emphasize the importance of calculating socially necessary labor. Why do you have to keep insisting on using the term law of value and wasting your time on semantic disputes? Why can't you just call it the law of socially necessary labor? This is what Comrade Xue Muqiao means by "avoiding unnecessary disputes."

But I really am not engaging in unnecessary disputes. In this sense, I do agree with Comrade Wang Sihua's statement: "Socially necessary labor is ultimately not the same thing as value." I objected earlier to this statement because he thinks that the calculation, regulation, and allocation of socially necessary labor in the communist society do not belong to the category of "value." But I also agree that we cannot equate the concept of "socially necessary labor" with the concept of "value." "Socially necessary labor" is basically a quantitative concept. It cannot express the qualitative aspect of the "value concept." In terms of what Engels said, "value is the relation of production costs (i.e., socially necessary labor — this author) to utility." This is the real reason why we have to pay attention to the concept of "value." To calculate socially necessary labor does not imply the less labor the better. If this was so, then it would be best not to labor at all. The reason for calculating socially necessary labor is to compare labor consumption with labor returns. Therefore, to pay attention to the concept of value in our socialist society is to pay attention to economic returns. It does not mean, as many economists think, the expression of value in a roundabout way (i.e., market competition). A long-term rejection in theory of the value concept in the communist society will lead to neglect of economic returns. (Rejection of the cost concept in the socialist economy and association of capital profit rate and investment returns with capitalism also result from this.)

When I wrote that paper in 1956, my understanding of the issue was not as clear as it is now. In that paper, I said that in the communist society it is not possible to just produce without calculating the labor costs involved. As to "whether this cost is called 'value' or directly as 'average socially necessary labor' is not that important."[30] The reader can tell that at the time, like Comrade Xue Muqiao, I was also reluctant to open up conceptual disputes. I thought that whatever terms were used was immaterial.

But Comrade Luo Gengmo seized upon this weakness of mine to launch his attack in his book Shehuizhuyi zhidu xia de shangpin he jiazhi wenti [Commodity and Value Under Socialism]:

> It is indeed a matter of relativity how a thing should be called. We do have a certain degree of freedom. But the people who come later, like us, certainly have less freedom than their predecessors. For we must respect and follow conventional usages of scientific terms and categories, unless what we talk about now has never been talked about before. In that case, it really doesn't matter what name is used to describe something. . . .[31]

I now accept Comrade Luo Gengmo's advice and agree that we "must respect and follow conventional usages of scientific terms and categories." But there is still one problem to be solved here. Who are the predecessors? Are they Marx and Engels? Or are they the writers of many papers, lectures, and textbooks in the past twenty to thirty years? Should we respect and follow the conventional usages of scientific terms and categories of the former, or should we follow the scientific terms and categories of the latter?

There is yet another problem to be solved. According to many economists, there will not be the category of "value" in communist political economy. Then does it mean that there will be no such concept as "value" in future human language? In the recent past, many economists started avoiding all "value" terms (especially costs, profit, capital profit, etc.) as if they wanted to eliminate the term "value" (whether as a noun or as a verb) from future dictionaries. This is indeed inconceivable!

A TENTATIVE COMMENT ON THE ROLE OF "VALUE" IN SOCIALIST AND COMMUNIST POLITICAL ECONOMY

According to my understanding of the category of value, I suggest that we should greatly elevate the position of this category in socialist political economy. But I do not think that value should be independently expressed as a law or a formula. Nor do I think that "value" should be understood as a law of the commodity economy.

If economic laws in general should not be expressed in isolation as a formula, then that is all the more reason why the law of value should not be expressed in isolation as a formula. But according to my understanding of the category of value in the socialist society, value should not be associated with commodities and commodity production in the same chapter either. Commodities and commodity production can be dealt with in one chapter. The law of value should underlie each and every chapter of socialist political economy. In other words, it should be expressed through an overall analysis of the socialist economy.

To avoid further misunderstanding, I am going to reiterate the following for the benefit of my critics. What I mean by the law of value here is not the regulating functions and influence exerted through the deviation of price from value that many economists usually emphasize. The concept of "value" that I am talking about here is the concept of value in a broad sense. It is what Engels said: "all that would be left in a communist society." The influence exerted by price deviation can be treated in relevant chapters as remnants from the past in the transitional period. (As we mentioned earlier, this influence is no longer very great. What we should emphasize now is exchange of equal values and direct expression of value through planned prices.)

But what steps should we follow to study the socialist economy? I think we should basically follow the steps taken by Marx in his writing of Capital. We should analyze the socialist economy in the same order that he analyzed the capitalist economy. In other words, we must first analyze the production process, then the circulation process, and finally the whole production process in the socialist society.

The direct object of study in Capital was obviously the capitalist society. But while analyzing the specific laws of the capitalist economy, Marx also analyzed the general laws of social production. These general laws are what Engels termed as "all that would be left" after eliminating the capitalist characteristics. These are what we should carefully study in Capital today.

In our struggle with the enemy in the old society, we always emphasized uniqueness, and not commonality and generality. But the ruling class always emphasized commonality and generality to cover up class antagonism. For example, they always talked about nationals and people in general. But we said there were no nationals and people in general. There were only workers, peasants, capitalists, landlords, bureaucrats, etc. The same applied to economic laws. We did not usually talk about economic laws in general. In the class society these general laws could not explain anything. But today in the socialist society, while getting rid of laws unique to the capitalist economy, we are also rejecting economic laws that are common and general to all economic systems. These are what Engels called "all that would be left in a communist society." This is as ridiculous as arguing that because we do not admit there are people in general in the class society, only people belonging to different classes, there will not be any people in the future communist society; nor will there still be a proletariat.

Marx's Capital started with the analysis of commodities – the cells that constitute the wealth of the capitalist society. I think that in socialist political economy, the first part should deal with the transitional period (primarily the three transformations) and ownership systems in the socialist society. The second part should deal with the socialist production process. The first chapter of part two should start with the material wealth of the socialist society and the cells that constitute this wealth – products. It should start with defining wealth.

Engels' instruction that ". . . .the balancing of useful effects and expenditure of labor would be all that would be left, in a communist society, of the concept of value as it appears in political economy" should be the one content of the first chapter in part two of socialist political economy. In this chapter, the natural economy (material economy) viewpoint that rejects the existence of the "value" concept in the communist society, and consequently treats the future communist society as a natural economy, in which there are only use value and no "value," and in which attention is paid only to material quantities and not to labor consumption, should be criticized. In this chapter, it should be explained that the socialist law of value with socially necessary labor as its concrete basis is in fact a law that promotes the development of productive forces and propels society forward by encouraging "the backward to catch up with the advanced, and the advanced to become more advanced."

Therefore, in this chapter, Marx's theory on the two factors of products (use value and value) and the two-fold character of labor (concrete labor and abstract labor) should be explained. In this chapter, it should be proved that after the opposition between mental labor and physical labor disappears, the difference between complex labor and simple labor will also disappear. But the difference between skilled and unskilled labor, namely the difference between socially necessary labor consumption and individual labor consumption, will always exist. This is also the perpetual basis for the progress of society and the movement to catch up with the advanced.

The next chapter should deal with economic accounting. But this economic accounting is not what people now generally understand as economic accounting. It does not mean independent accounting and quota management. It means the calculation of economic returns and saving of labor time. On this point, Marx said the following:

> Under the premise of common production, the determination of time is of primary importance. The less time is required by society to produce wheat and livestock, etc., the more time is available to produce other material and spiritual things. Like an individual, the overall development of society, and its enjoyment and activities, depends on how efficiently time is used. All economy boils down to the economy of time. Similarly, society must purposefully allocate its time in order to produce what meets its total needs. It must correctly allocate time like an individual in order to obtain knowledge in the proper proportions, and to satisfy the various requirements of its activities. Thus the economy of time and planned allocation of time among various production departments became the first economic law of common production. It can even be said that this is a law of a very high degree. But this is essentially different from assessing exchange value (labor or labor product) with labor time.[32]

This statement by Marx is very important for our present issue. This is also an issue that our practical and theoretical workers have overlooked. That is why I quoted this statement at length. The theoretical workers are particularly to blame for this neglect. Rejection of the "value" concept in the future society and in the internal relationship of the whole people ownership system cannot possibly lead to emphasis on economic returns and saving of labor time.

Furthermore, the last sentence in the quotation was even used by many economists as a reason to reject the existence of the "value" category in the communist society and the internal relationship of the whole people ownership system. After our explanation of "exchange value" above, we should now understand that there is an "essential difference" between the concept of "exchange value" and the concept of "value." This statement by Marx only rejected the existence of "exchange value." But the law of value was exalted as "the first economic law, or a law of a very high degree." What Marx referred to here as the first law, what he said in the third volume of Capital about "value determination continued to prevail," and the "concept of value" which Engels said "all that would be left in a communist society" can only be interpreted as meaning the same thing.

To analyze economic returns ("boils down to the economy of time") is the core of the law of value in the socialist society. Therefore, there should be a detailed explanation in this section of the two aspects of economic returns (the calculation of investment returns and labor productivity) and the methods for raising investment returns and labor productivity.

Because most economists in the past regarded the future economy as a natural economy, investment returns were treated as a capitalist economic category. In the mind of some people, investment returns, like economic accounting, are related to material incentives. And as such they exist because the communist consciousness of the masses is not high enough. This is utterly ridiculous. When the capitalist uses capital, he is very concerned with economic returns — investment returns. To distinguish ourselves from the capitalist, we call "capital" "capital fund." There is a certain advantage in using two different terms to distinguish between two different concepts. But we have gone too far in rejecting "investment returns" together with "capital." If even the capitalist takes care to husband the labor product expropriated from other people, how can the laboring people be careless in husbanding their own labor product created with their own blood and sweat by not paying attention to their investment returns? To take care of capital fund is to take care of labor. How can that be regarded as a capitalist economic category? The theoretical worker must be responsible for the neglect of investment returns in practical work. For this is the result of conceptual confusion. And this is an inevitable result of rejecting "the concept of value," and the two factors of products (use value and value). Therefore, I think it is necessary to discuss the nature and importance of investment returns in terms of theory and concept in this chapter. We should correct our misconception on this point. (I think there will be no need to talk about this point in great detail in the communist period because there will not be such conceptual confusion.)

When Chinese economists were studying labor productivity, some comrades wondered whether the issue of labor productivity should come under the scope of the "value" category. I think there is absolutely no doubt about it. Marx said: "The value of a commodity, therefore, varies directly as the quantity, and inversely as the productiveness, of the labor incorporated in it."[33] In other words, value and labor productivity are merely two aspects of the same thing. It all depends on from where it is approached. In terms of a mathematical formula, value and labor productivity are reciprocals. With product as denominator, and labor quantity as numerator, we have the formula for value; with product as numerator and labor quantity as denominator, we have the formula for labor productivity. Therefore, not only does labor productivity belong to the research scope of the category of "value," it is in fact inseparable from it.

After economic returns are discussed, money, price, and price formation in the socialist society should be dealt with.

Up to the present, economists have associated value, and hence money, with commodity production in the socialist society. According to our analysis above, under the regime of planned prices, exchange values that are associated with commodity exchange and market competition no longer exist. Therefore, money is no longer the original unit of account. It is a unit of account for the direct calculation of value. But as long as commodity exchange exists, money still serves as a medium of exchange.

Hence, planned prices in the socialist society are no longer prices that fluctuate continuously in millions and millions of exchanges. In other words, they are essentially direct expressions of values. The fact that our prices are not actually equal to values does not negate the essence that our planned prices are direct and not roundabout expressions of values. As to why prices are not equal to values, there are two reasons. One is largely historical (price differentials between industrial and agricultural products were even larger before Liberation. After Liberation, rising prices for agricultural products and falling prices for industrial products have narrowed but not eliminated these differentials); the other is that economic practitioners and theorists have not fully accepted the principle that prices in the socialist society not only should be based on values but also should directly express values. Therefore, theoretical explanations of prices and price formation are urgently needed at present. After collectivization (particularly after communalization), free market and spontaneous forces no longer exist or at least have been severely restrained. The path for the roundabout expression of value (i.e., through competition and repeated exchanges to establish market values) has been blocked. Planned prices have been established and implemented both in principle and in practice. But whether planned prices should be based on values (objective factor) and directly express values, or can be arbitrarily determined with no regard for values, remains an unsettled issue in principle.

Here we return once again to an old issue. Should value exert its influence through price that deviates from it, or through price that conforms with it? Should price be regarded as a means of accumulation, namely a means of redistributing national income, and hence a category in the circulation sphere, or should price and value be regarded as categories in the production sphere?

From the above-quoted instructions by Marx and Engels, we can see that they regarded value as a category in the production sphere Engels thought that even in the period of commodity economy, "the first application of value is the decision as to whether a thing ought to be produced at all.... Only then can one talk of the application of value to exchange." "Once private property is superseded, there can no longer be any question of exchange as it exists at present. The practical application of the concept of value will then be increasingly confined to the decision about production, and that is its proper sphere."

Even though private property has now been superseded, our economists are still reluctant to return "the concept of value" to "its proper sphere." Furthermore, our interests are focused on how to exert influence through deviation of prices from values. Consequently, price is now more and more treated as a category in the circulation sphere and a means of accumulation.

If we follow Engels' advice and allow "the concept of value to be increasingly applied to decision about production" as "its proper sphere," and make it participate in "formulating production plans," then, in Marx's words, "after the abolition of the capitalist mode of production, but still retaining social production, the determination of value continues to prevail... ultimately the bookkeeping encompassing all this, becomes more essential than ever."

Why did Marx mention bookkeeping here, and why did he think that bookkeeping would become more essential than ever? Obviously he did so in order to calculate labor expenditure accurately and to formulate production plans. We all know that inaccurate measurement units are not good measurement tools. Then price that often deviates from value is not an accurate tool to calculate labor (including material) expenditure either. Nor is it a good tool to formulate production plans and correctly solve production problems. Consequently, it cannot facilitate the return of the "concept of value" to "its proper sphere."

It is here that many questions are raised from the aspect of practical work. For example, can the total labor consumption of product, i.e., the value of product, be accurately calculated now? Will a wholesale adjustment of prices lead to confusion in prices? In particular, when prices are equal to values, where will socialist accumulation come from? etc.

It should be pointed out here that the most important thing to do is to clarify our understanding in theory and in principle. From the viewpoint of socialism and the future communism, is it better for prices to be equal to values, or is it better for prices to deviate from values? After the principle is established, it is a matter of procedure and method how prices can be brought closer to values. Further study can then be done. As to the method used to calculate the total labor consumption, I already indicated earlier that a solution has been found. Price adjustments must be done in a proper order so that market confusion can be avoided. Accumulation is the source of capital fund for socialist construction. In the adjustment of prices, the source of accumulation should be shifted from the indirect method to the direct method, and from a few departments to all production departments, to equalize the burden. Consequently, accumulation need not be affected by prices. This issue should be discussed in chapters on profit and taxation.

That prices should be equal to values is a principle that must be affirmed by us at present. But we need not absolutize this principle. We need not think that the price of any commodity under socialism should be absolutely equal to its value, without the slightest bit of deviation. On this point, the principle of equality between prices and values is similar to the principle of balance in the national economy. Balance is a principle. The task of our planning work is to achieve balance among the various departments of the national economy, and hence high speed development of production. But even so, balance is still relative. Lack of balance is more often the case.

Similarly, in principle, prices should be equal to values. In practice, prices often deviate from values for the following reasons. First, the value of product is continually falling owing to continually improving social labor productivity. But prices cannot be adjusted daily. Even planned prices in the socialist society cannot always be absolutely equal to values. Second, in the socialist period, only distribution according to labor is practicable. Output of means of production is not yet abundant. There are still different ownership systems. Production and demand are undergoing rapid changes. Moreover, there is still a lack of experience in planning and management work. Consequently, supply does not always match demand. Under this circumstance, planned and conscious deviation of prices from values within certain limits not only should be permitted, but is also necessary to discourage consumption of products in short supply and to encourage consumption of products with excess supply.

But these planned deviations of prices from values within certain limits are different in principle from the price policy that does not even accept value, that does not consider the calculation of value, and that sets prices according to subjective wishes.

We have been talking above about the equality of prices with values and assumed that prices are directly based on values. At present, some economists think that prices should be based on production prices.[b] How can such an economic category as production price still exist in the socialist society? There has indeed been dispute on this question among economists. In fact, this is another way of proposing capital profit. In the past, many economists thought that capital profit was also a capitalist concept. They thought that the calculation of profit in the socialist society should be based on product cost and not on capital fund. But there are more and more people who accept that profit should be calculated on the basis of capital fund. The acceptance of production price is the inevitable logical conclusion of the acceptance of capital profit. At the same time, only by accepting production price can the calculation of investment returns be implemented.

Marx mentioned production price in the second chapter of Capital, which deals with the circulation process. For production price is formed through market competition in the circulation process. Now that we have eliminated market competition, production price, like value, should be determined through planning. Therefore, the issue of production price should be discussed, to-

---

b) For a definition of production price, see Editor's Introduction in this volume, p. xvii. — K.K.F.

gether with price, in the study of the production process. Just as capitalist production price did not negate Marx's theory of value, so socialist production price will not negate value as its basis.

In this part on the production process, in addition to the above issues, how the value created by the staff and workers is to be divided into two parts should be studied, namely, one part goes to the laborers in the material production department, and the other part goes to meet social needs and accumulation. The different distribution principles in the communist society and the socialist society should be explained in detail, namely, distribution according to need and distribution according to labor. The form of distribution according to labor in the socialist society, wage form, should be analyzed in detail.

Finally, in this part on the production process, the question of agricultural production and rural people's communes should be analyzed. This is a concrete application of the previous chapters and sections to agriculture as a special sector of the national economy. Here, the special characteristics of agricultural production, investment returns and labor productivity in people's communes, the elimination of absolute rent, and the continued existence of differential rent after public ownership of land was established, the calculation and handling of differential rent, etc., should be analyzed in detail. Finally, the organizational structure, management system, and production planning of people's communes should also be analyzed and studied.

The planning system and management system of industry, transportation, and capital construction in the socialist society should also be studied in a separate chapter, particularly from the viewpoint of how the subjective activism of the various organizational levels and the whole people can be utilized, namely, how labor resources and material resources can be fully tapped to improve labor productivity and increase the production of material wealth.

Thus, in the first part on production process in socialist political economy, no particular reference is made to the law of value. But in every chapter, it can be seen that "the concept of value will be increasingly applied to the decision about production" as "its proper sphere."

The second part of socialist political economy should analyze the circulation process. According to my immature consideration, I think socialist reproduction should be analyzed in the third part. The second part should study primarily the circulation and inventory of consumer goods and producer goods. In the ten years since Liberation, state commerce agencies specializing in consumer goods have accumulated a lot of experience. In the past, there were also many studies on socialist commerce by economic researchers. But I think the most important and complex problem in the circulation process of the socialist society is the circulation of producer goods, what we call material resources allocation. But with the exception of those engaged in practical work in the business departments, those in theoretical research have paid little attention to this problem.

I think the circulation of producer goods is by far more important and complex than the circulation of consumer goods. This is not owing to a comparison between producer goods and consumer goods themselves, but to the following considerations.

Apart from the absence of private property and exploitation, the difference between the socialist economy and the capitalist economy is the replacement of market by planning, and the replacement of market allocation by plan allocation. Although our commerce in consumer goods is already state commerce under the socialist planned economy, basically the method of market allocation is still in use. It is still commerce, and many old methods and experiences of commerce are still adopted. But the allocation of producer goods is a brand new form of circulation. There is no similar experience in the old society. We can learn from the experience of other socialist countries, or we can create our own experience.

In the First Five-Year Plan period, our material resources management (primarily producer goods) was gradually centralized. Consequently, there was the problem of "excessive and inflexible control by Central agencies." After the experience of the First Five-Year Plan was summarized, the goal of decentralization was suggested. But after one year's decentralization, there were still many problems relating to material resources allocation. The power of allocation was once again centralized. Was the goal of decentralization wrong? I don't think the goal of decentralization was wrong. The goal of decentralization was correct. It should still be implemented in the future. We cannot conceive how a highly developed modern society can manage its economy in detail from one center, such as individually allocating hundreds and thousands of kinds of material resources. But in the process of decentralizing, what should definitely be decentralized and what should still be centrally controlled still requires further study.

Here we return again to an old issue: the socialist economy is not a natural economy of the primitive society. Here social wealth is no longer a bundle of different use values. Rather, they are a certain quantity of values. The planned economy of the socialist society must be subject to unified central guidance. Targets relating to abstract labor and value must be under strict central unified management. When management power is decentralized, and when independent accounting within the scope of simple reproduction is guaranteed to the enterprise, such unified central control will not lead to inflexibility. These centrally controlled targets are the financial targets relating to labor power (general abstract labor regardless of their specializations), capital fund (embodied labor), net output and profit. But physical targets relating to concrete labor and use values such as the variety of products (with the exception of a few nationwide items) should be decentralized. These targets can be handled through contracts and direct contacts among regions and enterprises. Some comrades think that recentralization of the material resources allocation system results from temporary shortages of certain supplies and is therefore not permanent. I also think that this is a temporary move. But these material shortages result exactly from inadequate control of the financial targets such as labor and capital fund.

Some problems in material resources allocation are not the inevitable results of decentralization. Rather, they result from disruptions of the original coordinations among enterprises. And these disruptions are contrary to the spirit of decentralization. For decentralization implies reduction of interferences with the internal relationship within enterprises and external relationships among enterprises that are contrary to objective economic laws. Disruptions of the original coordinations among enterprises implies exactly interferences that are contrary to objective economic laws.

Of course, circulation in the socialist society, particularly the allocation of producer goods, i.e., the replacement of anarchic capitalist market allocation by organized plan allocation, is a very important thing. It is a very complex and meticulous activity. Only the erroneous natural economy viewpoint leads to its oversimplification. What I said above was viewed from only one perspective. The purpose is to illustrate the point that without "the concept of value," we cannot even solve the circulation problem within the whole people ownership system (and this is a miniature of the future communist economy). The circulation problem under socialism is, of course, not confined to this one aspect. But this part of socialist political economy is the most ignored and least studied by the theorist.

In the third part of socialist political economy, the totality of the socialist production process should be studied. I think this part should include the total content of what is now called balance of the national economy (or comprehensive balance) based on Marx's theory of reproduction. Here comprehensive balance of the nation, as well as balance within and among regions, should be analyzed. This is a comprehensive analysis of the whole process of production, distribution, redistribution, circulation, and consumption. This comprehensive balance should be studied both from the material aspect and from the value aspect. Without the "concept of value," there is no way to observe the relationship between utility and production costs of individual products. In other words, there is no way to determine whether their production is economically justified. Without this "concept of value" in balancing the national economy, there is no genuine economic viewpoint in the national economy. From the viewpoint of national economic balance, the position taken by those who reject the "concept of value" and associate it only with material incentives and low communist consciousness is all the more ridiculous. In the comprehensive balance of the national economy, we can see that it is futile to reject the two factors of products (use values and value) in the socialist or even the communist society. The two-factor nature of products is especially obvious when the proportional development of the national economy is dislocated. For what is meant by proportional dislocation in planning work? It means that the contradiction between the value aspect and the material aspect of material wealth cannot be satisfactorily resolved. This unresolved contradiction can occur between producer goods and consumer goods, between accumulation and consumption, and among various departments. For example, the plan may call for allocating 80 percent of the increased wealth to expand heavy industry. In other words, what is needed mostly is producer goods. But 80 percent of the increased output may consist of agricultural and light industrial products. Therefore, if this mismatch is not remedied either through foreign trade or through other means, the implementation of such a plan will lead to shortage of producer goods and surplus of consumer goods.

It is not my intention to suggest a complete outline for socialist political economy. My purpose here is simply to illustrate the point that the "concept of value" is indispensable in any part of socialist or communist political economy. Without it there will be no political economy. And there is nothing economic about it.

I did not mention the law of planning and proportion. The reason is the same as not having one chapter for the "law of value" itself. If socialist political economy is woven through with the "concept of value," it should also be woven through with planning and proportion. In the first chapter of part one on production process in socialist political economy, when value is analyzed, it is already pointed out that the concept of value that "would be left in a socialist [sic] society" is no longer that value established in a roundabout way through anarchic market activities. Rather, it is planned value determined through rough calculation. Planning and proportion are, of course, the major topics in the discussion of the circulation process and particularly in the discussion of national economic balance.

The basic difference between the socialist economy and the capitalist economy, including the presence and absence of planning, should be explained in the initial introduction.

August 2, 1959
Jingji yanjiu [Economic Research], 1959, No. 9

NOTES

1. This and the previous quotation are from Xue Muqiao, "Commodity Production and Law of Value Under the Socialist System," Hongqi [Red Flag], 1959, No. 10, p. 20.

2. Marx, Capital, volume 1, People's Publishing Company, 1963, p. 9. [English translation based on the English edition published by Progress Publishers, Moscow, 1954, volume 1, p. 46. — K.K.F.]

3. "The gradual strengthening of the leadership position of the state economy and the gradual restricting of the law of value represent an important victory in our economic work in the past three, four years." Xue Muqiao, "The Function of the Law of Value in China's Economy," Xuexi [Study], 1953, No. 9, as quoted in Wo guo jingji xuejie guanyu shehuizhuyi zhidu xia shangpin jiazhi he jiage wenti lunwen xuanji [Collected Essays on Commodity, Value, and Prices Under Socialism by Chinese Economists], edited by the Political Economy Group, Institute of Economics, Chinese Academy of Sciences, published by Scientific Publishing Company.

4. Ibid., pp. 184-85.

5. Jingji yanjiu [Economic Research], 1959, No. 2, p. 9.

6. Hongqi, 1959, No. 10, p. 19 and p. 20.

7. Jingji yanjiu, 1959, No. 1, p. 19. Underlines added by this author.

8. Ibid.

9. Ibid.

10. *Hongqi*, 1959, No. 10, p. 20.

11. Wang Sihua, "Some Personal Observations on Several Questions Relating to Commodity Production and the Law of Value under Socialism," *Jingji yanjiu*, 1959, No. 1, p. 21.

12. For a detailed discussion of this point, see "Gross Output and Related Issues," originally published in *Tongji gongzuo* [Statistical Work], 1957, No. 13, p. 8. [See Chapter 2 in this volume. — K.K.F.]

13. Wang Yanan, "The Functions of the Law of Value in China's Socialist Economy," *Renmin ribao* [People's Daily], January 17, 1959. Wang Yanan, "Fully Exploit the Functions of the Law of Value in China's Socialist Economy," *Renmin ribao*, May 15, 1959. Underlines added by this author.

14. Marx, *Capital*, volume 1, 1963, People's Publishing Company, p. 11. [English translation based on the English edition published by Progress Publishers, Moscow, 1954, volume 1, p. 48. — K.K.F.]

15. Sun Yefang, "Build Planning and Statistics on the Law of Value," *Jingji yanjiu*, 1956, No. 6. [See Chapter 1 in this volume. — K.K.F.]

16. Engels, *Anti-Duhring*, in *Complete Works of Marx and Engels*, People's Publishing Company, volume 20, 1971, p. 334. [English translation based with minor modifications on *Anti-Duhring*, trans. by Emile Burns, International Publishers, New York, 1939, pp. 337-38 — K.K.F.]

17. Marx, *Capital*. Underlines added by this author. [Sun translated this passage into Chinese from the 1952 Russian edition. No page number was given. English translation based on the English edition published by Progress Publishers, Moscow, 1954, volume 1, p. 54 — K.K.F.]

18. Marx, *Capital*. Underlines added by this author. [Sun translated this passage into Chinese from the 1952 Russian edition. No page number was given. English translation based on the English edition published by Progress Publishers, Moscow, 1954, volume 1, pp. 84-85 — K.K.F.]

19. Xue Muqiao, "Some Comments on Commodity Production and the Law of Value," *Jingji yanjiu*, 1959, No. 1, p. 19.

20. Ibid. While Comrade Muqiao objects to "mere conceptual disputes" on the one hand, he is engaged on the other in semantic exercises about the functions of the law of value. To differentiate between the functions the law of value performs in the socialist society and the capitalist society, economists have invented many functions, such as "regulating function," "impact function," "major function," "certain function," the above-mentioned "tool function," etc. Can we really see any essential difference among these "functions?" For example, in the paper from which I quoted earlier, Comrade Wang Sihua says after disagreeing with me and Comrade Zhongjin: "In state enterprises under whole people ownership, the law of value only performs the function of an accounting tool, it plays a certain function only in the cooperative economy under collective ownership." The question is: Is "tool function" not part of "certain function"? Can "certain function" also include "tool function"?

21. Marx, *Capital*, volume 3, People's Publishing Company, 1975, p. 963. [English translation based on the English edition published by Progress Publishers, Moscow, 1959, volume 3, p. 851 — K.K.F.]

22. Hu Jichuang, "The 'Determination of Value' Is Not the Same as the Law of Value," Jingji yanjiu, 1959, No. 7, p. 55.

23. Jingji yanjiu, 1956, No. 6, p. 35. [See Chapter 1 in this volume, p. 16. – K.K.F.]

24. Luo Gengmo, Shehuizhuyi zhidu xia de shangpin he jiazhi wenti [Commodity and Value Under Socialism], Scientific Publishing Company, p. 120.

25. Jingji yanjiu, 1959, No. 7, p. 57.

26. Engels, Anti-Duhring, People's Publishing Company, 1974, p. 340. [English translation based on Anti-Duhring, trans. by Emile Burns, International Publishers, New York, 1939, p. 338. – K.K.F.] Based on this footnote and the following Engels' quotation from his 1844 statement, Academician Si-te-lu-mi-lin, also confirmed in his On the Road to Building Communism (Chinese edition published by Joint Publishing Company in 1959) that "it is not simple to plan without the aid of value." Si-te-lu-mi-lin also thought that Engels "meant exchange value" in his "without the intervention of the famous 'value'" statement in Anti-Duhring. His conclusion agrees completely with that in my 1956 paper. [See Chapter 1 in this volume. – K.K.F.] But at that time, I did not notice this footnote of Engels'. The moral here is that we can never read carelessly, especially when reading classical works. Even a footnote should not be overlooked. We can see here how theoretically valuable these two just quoted footnotes by Marx and Engels are!

27. Engels, "Outlines of a Critique of Political Economy," in Complete Works of Marx and Engels, volume 1, People's Publishing Company, 1956, p. 605. Underlines added by this author. [English translation based on Karl Marx, Frederick Engels, Collected Works, volume 3, Progress Publishers, Moscow, 1975, p. 426 – K.K.F.]

28. Marx never treated the deviation of price from value and the influence this deviation exerts as the whole law of value. On the contrary, we must admit that all the economic works by Marx, especially Capital, volume 3, deal with the law governing the existence and operation of value.

29. Marx, Capital, volume 1, 1975, Chinese edition, p. 98. [English translation based on the English edition published by Progress Publishers, Moscow, 1954, volume 1, p. 85. – K.K.F.]

30. Jingji yanjiu, 1956, No. 6, p. 31. [See Chapter 1 in this volume, p. 10. – K.K.F.]

31. Luo Gengmo, Shehuizhuyi zhidu xia de shangpin he jiazhi wenti [Commodity and Value Under Socialism], p. 109.

32. Marx, Money, one of his 1857-58 economic manuscripts. It was translated by Comrade Dong Wenqiao and proofread by Comrade Liu Xiaoran. Underlines added by this author. [English translation here based on this Chinese translation. – K.K.F.]

33. Marx, Capital, volume 1, People's Publishing Company, 1975, pp. 53-54. [English translation based on the English edition published by Progress Publishers, Moscow, volume 1, 1954, p. 48. – K.K.F.]

4

On the Financial and Economic System within the Whole People Ownership Economy (Research Report)

1. THE STATUS OF SYSTEMS IN SOCIALIST POLITICAL ECONOMY

The issue of the financial and economic system has been raised by the Center and Chairman Mao for a number of years. The business departments are more concerned with this issue. Their concern is to reform existing administrative and management systems through solving current practical problems. Economists have not paid much attention to this issue as a research topic. Or they simply treat it as a problem of management system. Furthermore, some economists regard research efforts by economists on systems of economic management and suggestions to expand enterprise power as revisionist. In recent years, debates on economic systems are frequently published in foreign economic journals. But they treat it as a problem of law (the relation between civil law and economic law), and not as a problem of political economy. However, the financial and economic management system is not only or is not primarily a problem of law; it is also an important theoretical problem in socialist political economy.

Therefore, I think Comrade [Li] Fuchun's remarks in this connection in the most recent conference on industrial and transportation work have tremendous theoretical significance in socialist political economy. He suggested that we should replace the issue of ownership with the issue of system within the whole people ownership economy, and treat the latter and the interpersonal and distribution relationship in the labor process (direct production process) as one of the major aspects of our research on production relationships.

There is a limit to how far we can go in the reform of the ownership system, at least with respect to a specific period.

With the exception of a possible change from whole people ownership in one country to whole people ownership on the whole earth when communism finally triumphs over the whole world, it is difficult at the present time to conceive how whole people ownership can be changed any further. But the economic management system of the whole society, like the interpersonal and distribution relationships in the labor process (direct production process), improves and changes continuously.

The financial and economic system is not a distribution relationship. It is also different from the interpersonal relationship in the labor process (direct production process), i.e., division of labor and management system within an enterprise. The issue of the financial and economic system is an issue of operation and management power. It involves the rights to possess, use, and control which are parts of the rights bundle of ownership discussed by legal scholars. One foreign LL.D. thinks that from time immemorial people have realized that whoever possesses the rights to possess, use, and control becomes the owner. But after the laboring people seize political power, things are completely different. Under whole people ownership, the rights to possess, use, and control form one entity, while the right of ownership forms another entity. State enterprises only exercise the rights to possess, use, and control state assets permanently assigned to them according to their activities and needs. These assets are still owned by the state.

It is not correct to say that in societies with private ownership the right of ownership is never separated from the rights to possess, use, and control. In Capital, volume 3, chapter 23 ("Interest and Enterprise Profit"), Marx discussed at length the separation between money capitalists and industrial capitalists, i.e. between owners and users. In old China, there existed in many regions the distinction between bottom right and surface right over farmland. The so-called bottom right referred to the ownership right; the surface right referred to the use right. The bottom right and the surface right could once be bought and sold separately. (It is incorrect to say the owner of whole people assets is the state. If they are called whole people assets, then their owner should be the people – note by this author, November 1978.)

Still, by distinguishing ownership right from the rights to possess, use, and control under whole people ownership, this LL.D. provided indirect support for our topical interest: under whole people ownership, when the question of ownership is resolved, operation and management power should replace ownership right as the primary aspect of the three aspects of the production relationship in socialist political economy research.

2. THE CORE ISSUE OF THE FINANCIAL AND ECONOMIC SYSTEM IS THE ISSUE OF OPERATION AND MANAGEMENT POWER; THE LINE OF DEMARCATION BETWEEN BIG AND SMALL POWER, AND BETWEEN FLEXIBLE CONTROL AND STRUCTURED FREEDOM IS PRIMARILY THE LINE OF DEMARCATION BETWEEN EXPANDED REPRODUCTION AND SIMPLE REPRODUCTION

The core issue in the financial and economic management system is an issue involving the power and responsibility of the enterprise as an independent accounting unit and its relationship with the state. In other words, it is an issue concerning the operation and management power of enterprises. Other issues in the system, such as the relationship between the Center and the localities, between vertical and regional leadership, etc., can be easily resolved once the power of the enterprises is resolved.

The socialist economy is a highly socialized economy built on public ownership of the means of production. It is composed of millions of independent accounting enterprises. Each enterprise is a basic unit in socialized production. Among them there is a close division of labor and coordination. Any change in this relationship initiated by one enterprise will affect many other enterprises. This relationship is not one that would occur in a natural economy, such as the technical division of labor in a workshop, or the labor division that existed in primitive communist tribes and feudal manors, as envisioned by political economy theorists who deny the existence of broadly defined political economy. Nor is it like one that would exist in a commodity economy which is governed by the spontaneous forces of market value. How to handle the relationship among independent accounting enterprises is an important issue in socialist economic management.

The Center and Chairman Mao not only raised the issue of the financial and economic system long ago, they also suggested a correct principle to resolve it. Chairman Mao once said that within the broad scope of national life, we should create a political phase in which there is centralism as well as democracy, discipline, freedom, unified will, personal ease of mind, and liveliness. The concretization of this general political principle in the financial and economic management system requires the implementation of the principle of "centralize big power, decentralize small power," and "flexible control and structured freedom." After summing up the experience from the First Five-Year Plan and the beginning of the Second Five-Year Plan, the Center raised the issue of decentralizing power to address problems arising from excessive and inflexible control exercised by the financial and economic organs at the Center. As a result of some power decentralization in financial and economic work in recent years, some degree of chaos emerged during the Great Leap Forward. Consequently, the issue of centralizing some power was raised last year. This is entirely necessary and correct, given the situation. But it is necessary to clarify whether this is retrogression and whether the Center's opposition to excessive and inflexible control and the idea of power decentralization of several years ago are incorrect. What is "inflexibility" and what is "flexibility"? What "big power" should be centralized and what "small power" should be decentralized? Is the question of "big power" vs "small power" merely a matter of quantity (e.g., matters involving more than a certain amount of yuan belong to big power; matters involving less belong to small power, etc.)? It is essential to solving concrete problems and preventing conceptual confusion that these questions be clarified.

I think the demarcation between "big power" and "small power," and between "inflexibility" and "flexibility," is the demarcation between expanded reproduction and simple reproduction. Anything that relates to expanded reproduction comes under the state's "big power." Over these things the state must exercise strict control. Lack of control or lax control will lead to chaos. Anything that relates to simple reproduction comes under the "small power" of enterprises. Meddling in these things by the state will lead to inflexibility. According to Marx, simple reproduction involves a restoration of the original value after each turnover of the enterprise capital; expanded reproduction involves not only a restoration of the original value of the capital after each turnover, but also an increase in capital.

For example, the state sets up an enterprise with capital valued at 1 billion labor hours. This 1 billion labor hours of value includes not only the physical plant, equipment, and all necessary raw materials for production, but also wages needed to pay the staff and workers. Matters related to the preservation of the value of this

1 billion labor hours, such as the renovation of buildings and equipment, maintenance of raw materials for production, the payroll for staff and workers, etc., are the minimum responsibilities of the enterprise leadership and all the staff and workers. These are matters of ordinary business that they attend to year in and year out. These matters should be handled by the enterprise itself. There is no need for the state to reapprove every time something is done.

With technology continually improving and labor productivity continually increasing, even the simple reproduction of capital in value terms in the enterprise results in expanded reproduction in physical terms. Take the above example of the enterprise that is set up with capital valued at 1 billion labor hours. If the turnover cycle is ten years, and in these ten years the average social labor productivity increases by 100 percent, then the simple reproduction of capital value (in effect the quantity or efficiency of enterprise buildings, equipment, raw materials) will also increase by 100 percent. Consequently, the physical quantity of its product will also increase by 100 percent. But as long as it is within the scope of the simple reproduction of capital in value terms, this expanded reproduction in physical terms should still be within the "small power" of the enterprise. This is because, first, the responsibility of the enterprise to maintain the original value of the capital entrusted to it by the state cannot be separated from its responsibility to improve technology and labor productivity and consequently the efficiency of the original capital; second, if labor productivity improves at basically the same rate among various industries in the whole society, expanded reproduction in physical terms that is within the scope of simple reproduction of capital in value terms will not lead to imbalance in the national economy. Therefore, the power within this scope can be completely delegated to the enterprise without any fear of chaos.

But the responsibility of the enterprise lies not only in maintaining the value of the original capital, but also in increasing its value. That is to say, it must produce profit for the state and the society. This profit should be used either to build new enterprises, expand old enterprises (expanded reproduction in value terms), or to build up social welfare, science, culture, education, and health facilities. These things cannot and should not be handled by one enterprise alone. Therefore, enterprise profit should be sent to the state. And its disposal should come under the big power of the state. (In order to encourage enterprises with good performance, a portion of the profit which is above the society average can be allocated to the enterprise as bonus.)

What we do now is different from this. For example, depreciation charges only replenish the original capital. They are not newly created value. According to the current practice, however, the capital depreciation fund of fixed assets is treated as a part of state revenues. The enterprise controls only major repair fees. The depreciation rate is very low, and consequently the depreciation period for fixed assets is long.[1] This creates false profit. This system also has the following institutional drawbacks.

First, the state is managing business that is within the scope of simple reproduction which the enterprise should be responsible for. In fact, the annual appropriations assigned to enterprises by the state to buy additional equipment and update technology are not necessarily less than the capital depreciation fund sent to the state by enterprises. But these funds must be applied for individually by enterprises and approved by the state. This back and forth traffic not only increases paper work, but also, more importantly, inhibits the freedom of enterprises. This restriction discourages enterprise initiative and long-term planning on matters within the scope of simple reproduction, especially the renewal of fixed assets. As I understand it, the common problem faced by the leadership in state enterprises is a lack of control over their own fixed assets. This is because what we and all socialist countries have is basically the system of uncompensated allocation of fixed assets that has been in effect in the Soviet Union for several decades. This system results in waste of fixed assets, especially equipment. This fixed assets allocation system plus state financial subsidy to unprofitable enterprises effectively reduces the status of enterprises as independent accounting units.[a]

Second, because enterprises are not responsible for the renewal

a) Uncompensated allocation of fixed assets is related to unified revenues and unified expenditures in financial management in which all profits and most depreciation charges of state enterprises are to be turned over to the state treasury. And almost all capital expenditures, including quota circulating capital of state enterprises, are to be financed interest free by the state treasury regardless of individual enterprise performance. See Xue Muqiao, Current Economic Problems in China, ed. and trans. by K. K. Fung (Boulder, Colorado: Westview Press, 1982), pp. 85, 111, and Editor's Introduction. — K.K.F.

of fixed assets (especially equipment), they do not have an overall plan. The mechanical separation of capital construction from major repair within the scope of fixed asset renewal (i.e., simple reproduction) hinders technological improvement. This was especially true before the Great Leap Forward. There were many unreasonable restrictions governing the use of major repair fund; for example, major repairs of fixed assets could not be used to disguise value augmentation. This seriously affected equipment renewal and technological advance.[b] During the Great Leap Forward, this unreasonable system was partly broken up. This year, after opposition to laxity in the financial system was raised, the old restriction governing the use of major repair fund for capital construction was reinstituted. In fact, there is an unhealthy tendency among enterprises to ignore repairs of existing equipment and concentrate on new capital construction. Many factors are responsible for this tendency. One of them is the fixed assets allocation system. I think the first thing to do is to distinguish clearly between simple reproduction and expanded reproduction. Serious attention should be paid to the distinction between capital construction and major repair within the scope of simple reproduction. If we do not do so, we will end up where we start.

Third, because the state gets involved in matters within the scope of simple reproduction which should be managed by hundreds of thousands of independent accounting enterprises, it is bogged down by daily routine and is remiss in important planning for long-term national construction, namely, matters within the scope of expanded reproduction and balancing the national economy.

After power is divided between the state and enterprises, relationships between the Center and local authorities and between vertical leadership and regional leadership can be easily resolved. Not even local authorities can interfere with matters involving the "small power" of enterprises. But local authorities can exercise supervision and inspection over all enterprises in behalf of the state. Party work and mass work in all enterprises must of course be under the leadership of local authorities. The demarcation between central enterprises and local enterprises does not depend on the size of enterprise capital or the number of staff and workers. Rather, it depends on the supply and marketing relationship and the coordination relationship among enterprises. Local

b) See Chapter 2 in this volume, pp. 32-34. — K.K.F.

enterprises are those that have supply, marketing, and coordination relationships within a region. Those that have relationships outside the region are not local enterprises. The "big power" of local enterprises belongs to local authorities, and the "big power" of central enterprises belongs to the Center. I believe that if enterprises manage matters relating to simple reproduction, local authorities manage Party and mass work, and banks supervise financial management, then the central industrial ministries will only have to deal with planning and research on and introduction of advanced industrial technology. They will not be bogged down with routine administration.

3. THE MATERIAL RESOURCES SYSTEM IS ANOTHER IMPORTANT ISSUE IN THE FINANCIAL AND ECONOMIC SYSTEM. THE KEY TO SOLVING THE PROBLEM IS TO EMPHASIZE LABOR DIVISION AND COORDINATION AMONG ENTERPRISES AND THE CONTRACT SYSTEM

The most critical problem in the financial and economic system is the material resources supply and marketing system.[c] But once we realize that the socialist planned economy is not only different from the commodity economy, but also different from the natural economy, and we determine the power of enterprises (i.e., the power to manage independently all economic matters within the scope of simple reproduction), half of this problem is solved. The other half of the problem is to emphasize the coordination relationship among enterprises, emphasize the contract system, and distinguish between "big power" and "small power" and between flexible control and structured freedom in this aspect.

I think all changes from existing and traditional coordination relationships and supply and marketing relationships, changes in the production orientation of enterprises, and the organization of supply, marketing, and coordination relationships for new enterprises come under the "big power" of the state. Even local governmental authorities do not have the power to interfere with them. But within the original coordination relationship, and supply and marketing relationship, and within the original production orientation and scope, enterprises should be allowed to draw up periodic supply and marketing contracts and negotiate supply and

c) Material resources here refer to producer goods. — K.K.F.

marketing quantity, variety, and specifications without interference from the state or local authorities. Once contracts are drawn up, all parties must abide by them. Any dispute will be dealt with by the planning departments at a higher level. The implementation of this principle will ensure flexible control and structured freedom.

The socialist economy is more socialized and more complex than the capitalist economy. There exists a close coordination relationship among almost one million enterprises. Even a shortfall in the supply of something as insignificant as pine resin or straw rope could disrupt or stop work in large industrial and transportation enterprises. There may be irrationalities in the original or traditional coordination relationships, but widespread chaos will result if there is no overall arrangement before the relationships are changed. Therefore, any change in the coordination relationship must be approved by the higher level (changes in coordination among large regions must be approved by the Center, those within a large region must be approved by the central bureau, and those within a province must be approved by the province). Abiding by supply and marketing contracts must be regarded as the paramount responsibility of enterprises to the state and society.

Our situation is just the opposite. On the one hand, local administration departments or even enterprises themselves can, without the concurrence of their coordinating parties and with no regard for alternative supply and marketing arrangements, change their production orientation at will (for example, when one plant changes from manufacturing insulating porcelain to refractory bricks, the coordinating parties are caught short of these parts for their turbines and generators. When one sewing needle plant stops producing needles, the livelihood of many people in the nation is adversely affected). On the other hand, however, our state planning agencies and economic management agencies make a great effort to manage supply and marketing problems among hundreds and thousands of independent enterprises which are within the scope of simple reproduction and can thus be solved through direct contracts among them. This is why goods ordering conferences attended by thousands and thousands of people have to be organized.

To ensure that enterprises will not stop work while waiting for material supplies and that their supply and marketing work can proceed smoothly, it is also necessary to establish a material inventory system for the state and the enterprises themselves. No plans, no matter how scientific and exact, can anticipate all conditions. Without the necessary material inventory, many enterprises (whose capital is many many times the value of the necessary material inventory that is in short supply) must go into an inventory status. What is worse, their most valuable productive forces, i.e., the labor force, is wasted. Therefore, it is very important to establish a material inventory system and to determine the necessary inventory quotas for various material supplies with the aid of scientific calculation and practical experience. Not only will normal production operation be affected when the necessary material inventory is not available, but also the rate of socialist construction will also be affected when the inventory is so big that social capital is idled.

4. SEVERAL RESERVATIONS

There are two reservations in adopting the above-mentioned enterprise management system and material management system.

The first reservation is whether the profit maximizing capitalist management mentality will be encouraged after independent accounting and contract relationships among enterprises are emphasized. That is, will enterprises produce only products with big profit and ignore needed products that promise little profit?

I think this reservation is unnecessary. This is because, first, major business orientations are determined by the higher level. And traditional supply and marketing relationships cannot be changed without the approval of all the concerned parties and the higher level. There is thus little room for capitalist-type speculation and manipulation; second, there are two reasons why some products are more profitable. One reason is that some enterprises become good at management by improving their technology and consequently reducing their per unit labor consumption below the average socially necessary labor. This profit is obtained through the subjective efforts of the staff and workers. We should not restrict this profit. Instead, we should encourage it because this is profit borne of raising labor productivity and developing social production. Another reason is that prices are unreasonable. Because prices are not determined according to average socially necessary labor, products for which prices are higher than the socially necessary labor produce profit. Products for which prices are lower than the socially necessary labor produce no profit. Therefore, as long as prices are determined correctly, there is no room for this type of speculation and manipulation. And consequently this source of disorder will not occur. As the principles governing price formation and methods for calculating labor costs are separate problems, we will not discuss them here.

The second reservation is whether chaos in capital fund management and capital construction will result after enterprises are entrusted with the depreciation fund and assume the responsibility for renewing fixed assets. I don't think the cause of the current chaos in capital construction lies in the renewal of existing fixed assets that are within the scope of simple reproduction of value. Rather it lies in the construction of new enterprises. The chaos does not come from enterprises' having too much responsibility for the capital fund entrusted to them by the state. Rather, it comes from enterprises' not having the total power and responsibility of an independent accounting unit. Enterprises therefore always want to have more than what they need, whether it is with respect to investment, equipment, or material supplies. With regard to the management of depreciation fund, the state should establish some system and supervise its use through bank control over depreciation fund. But these regulations and systems should not be too strict.

5. THE DUALITY OF VALUE AND USE VALUE AND THE FINANCIAL AND ECONOMIC SYSTEM

As mentioned above, with increasing labor productivity, simple reproduction in value terms is in effect expanded reproduction in physical terms or in use value terms. Here, we can see that value and use value are not only different in quality, but also different in the direction in which the quantity moves, sometimes even moving in opposite directions. The development of labor productivity implies that the physical output produced by a unit of labor time increases. But the labor required to produce the same unit of product, i.e., value, decreases. In the comprehensive balance of the national economy, we can often see an inseparable unity of contradictions between value and use value which differ in quality and the movement of their quantity. This happens, for example, in the relationships between consumption and accumulation, between producer goods and consumer goods, and among various economic departments. From the viewpoint of the internal relationships under whole people ownership, there are theoretical disagreements on whether a product has both value and use value. Most theorists tend to deny the existence of this duality. I do not intend to go into this here. All I want to do is discuss concrete problems in the financial and economic system from this aspect.

Since value and use value are two inseparable aspects of all economic problems, it is necessary to deal with both aspects when we deal with economic problems. This is because cost effectiveness involves simply a comparison between what Engels called labor expenditure and useful effects. Labor expenditure is value, and useful effects are use value, i.e., physical output. If expenditure is controlled while effects are neglected, or if effects are emphasized while expenditure is neglected, economic principles are violated. Only the general line of achieving greater, faster, and better results at lower costs is a balanced approach.

But value targets and use value targets serve different functions. Value is a fruit of abstract labor. And the use value of different products with different specifications manifests many different kinds of concrete labor. While we cannot ignore concrete matters, they degenerate easily into trivialities over which excessive control could be exercised. In our present system of planning targets, there are more physical targets than value targets (gross product or net product at constant prices are both physical targets), and there is more concern for output quantity than capital fund management. Many economists have a traditional dogmatic attitude toward the truth that the purpose of the socialist economy is not to pursue profit. It is correct that our goal is not profit but the growth of material wealth. But to achieve this goal, we must reduce cost to increase benefit. Therefore profit is still a necessary means to our end. The capitalists are very smart. To achieve their chosen end — profit — they are very careful about their means. That is, they pay attention to production efficiency and product variety and specification (product quality). As a result, they succeed in achieving their goal. We sometimes do the opposite thing. We only see the end we are after — material wealth — but we do not pay attention to the means for achieving our end — increased profit for the state and society. Consequently, results are not as good as we expect.

Another matter in the financial and economic system also deserves our consideration. That is, planning agencies that are primarily concerned with physical targets (use value) and financial agencies that are primarily concerned with value targets belong to two independent systems. This is a carbon copy of the Russian method. But I think this system is not as good as the system of a unified financial and economic commission we had soon after Liberation.

We must pay attention to the following phenomenon in our practice: In the past few years, the planning department and the economic management department often experienced material shortages. In fact, material inventory was on its way down. But there was a financial surplus year after year. This dislocation between the financial account (value) and the material account (use value) indicated a dislocation between value targets and physical targets in management method and a separation of the financial system from the planning system in the management system.

Why did the Soviet Union adopt this system that separated the planning agencies from the financial agencies for forty years? This was inseparable from the influence exercised by the natural economy position in socialist political economy in the past several decades. In the 1920s, the natural economists regarded the production relation in the socialist planned economy as simple as the technical division of labor in a workshop or a self-sufficient economy in a primitive communist society or feudal manor. Therefore, they denied the existence of socialist political economy. In 1930, the denial of the existence of socialist political economy was overturned after Lenin's comments on Bukharin's On Transitional Economy (Lenin thought that political economy still existed in the socialist society) were published. But the theoretical basis of this position — natural economism — has not been criticized. Instead, it exercises deep-rooted influence over current theory and practice. This is first of all manifested in the denial of the two-fold character of labor (concrete labor and abstract labor) and the two factors of products (use value and value). When objective conditions forced the natural economy school to admit the existence of the law of value, they merely related "value" to the existence of different ownership systems and the existence of commodities. They even went to the other extreme by emphasizing the law of market value and the material incentives induced by the deviation of prices from values. They exaggerated the commodity nature of the planned economy and even regarded the commodity economy as the essence of the planned economy.

As a result of this natural economy viewpoint, the system of planning targets is heavily biased toward physical targets, and prices (especially internal allocation prices) are greatly divorced from values. Consequently, interdepartmental balance tends to rely on material balance because balance in value terms no longer reflects the real conditions.

Under the influence of this natural economism, there is an independence between financial agencies and planning agencies. The dominant thought in Soviet finance considers finance as a representation of the commodity relationship and money relationship. And there would be no finance if there are no commodities or money. In fact, the essence of our socialist financial work at present has been to make deductions from the social product, just as was suggested by Marx in his A Critique of the Gotha Program. In other words, the financial agency has become an agency of distribution and redistribution of the national income and has nothing to do with the nature of commodities and money (the original meaning of money).

Under the guidance of this natural economy thought, work in the circulation of products has been neglected. Even the existence of such a category as product circulation is denied because only commodities need to be circulated. "Product circulation" is considered a joke. Consequently, material allocation is emphasized in the internal relationships under whole people ownership. And the contract and coordination relationships among hundreds and thousands of independent accounting enterprises are neglected.

While we are studying the financial system, it is also necessary to criticize and reject this natural economy thinking.

June 2, 1961

NOTE

1. Before World War I, capitalist economic crises occurred about once every ten years and lasted for about three years each. Therefore, the whole cycle, i.e., the renewal period of capital, lasted for about thirteen years. After World War II, this cycle was shortened to about five years. But the depreciation period in our industrial enterprises lasts for about twenty-five years. The depreciation period in transportation industries is even longer. [See also Chapter 2 in this volume, pp. 31-32. — K.K.F.]

5

An Introduction to Circulation

1. PRODUCTION AND EXCHANGE; EXCHANGE AND CIRCULATION; EXCHANGE AND COMMODITY EXCHANGE; CIRCULATION AND COMMODITY CIRCULATION [1]

Exchange does not create the differences between the spheres of production, but brings what are already different into relation, and thus converts them into more or less inter-dependent branches of the collective production of an enlarged society.[2]

Circulation is merely a particular phase of exchange or exchange regarded in its totality.

Since exchange is simply an intermediate phase between production, distribution, which is determined by production, and consumption; since consumption is moreover itself an aspect of production, the latter obviously comprises also exchange as one of its aspects.[3]

In talking about commodity circulation, Marx again said: "Circulation is a perpetual movement of commodities, though always of different commodities, and each commodity makes but one move."[4]

Engels:

...production and the accompanying exchange of products are the basis of all social systems. In every historical society, the distribution of products and the accompanying social classes and castes are determined by what this society produces, how it produces and how it exchanges what it produces.[5]

But, as was repeatedly mentioned in our study of the production process, the "natural economy viewpoint" that was popular in the past half century among socialist political economy circles holds that only commodities can be exchanged. And there will be no ex-

exchange once commodities disappear. Nor is there such a thing as circulation as "exchange in general."

Recently, a Russian economist, A. Ke-liu-qie-fu, said in a paper published in a relatively unknown journal of a business college (views such as his are not easily accepted for publication in well-known journals dominated by the "natural economy viewpoint"):

> There is a deep-rooted view in our economic works that circulation can only be thought of as commodity circulation. Other than commodity circulation, there cannot be any other kinds of circulation. According to this view, it follows that only when circulation is regarded as commodity circulation can it constitute a special stage of social production.[6]

This "natural economy viewpoint" also exists in China's economics circle. The ideas of foreign economists inevitably affect the ideas of China's economists. We can tell that from the following incidents.

First, in China, as in other countries, socialist political economy is primarily concerned with problems arising from the production process. As far as problems relating to the circulation process are concerned, only exchange of consumer goods among different ownership systems (state, collective, and individual consumers) is discussed. Circulation within the whole people ownership system, and circulation of producer goods, is not discussed at all. On the rare occasions when the provision of producer goods is mentioned in schools and in newspapers and journals, it is mentioned as a concrete problem of administrative organization in planning or production management. It is not mentioned as an independent economic process in social reproduction that is independent of the direct production process and yet inseparable from it because of their mutual constraint. And no matter how important commodity exchange among different ownership systems is in the socialist economy as an initial stage of the communist society, it is still a relic from the past (private ownership and commodity exchange). It is not born and bred from the production relation under whole people ownership. Therefore, if we limit our discussion to the commerce of consumer goods, then circulation, like commodity exchange, is only a phenomenon in the initial stage of communism. There is no such category and concept as "circulation" from the viewpoint of the basic production relationship of the socialist economy and whole people ownership.

Second, in recent years many people have held that socialist political economy should be written by analyzing objective economic processes. But difficulties are encountered in trying to answer the questions of what the circulation process is and whether it exists at all. This shows that we have overlooked the circulation process in the past. Only in recent years is the question of whether the circulation process exists in the whole people ownership system raised. But if there is no circulation process, no exchange, and particularly no product exchange as a medium, then social production itself becomes isolated and unrelated economic activities. Thus it is not surprising that so far works on socialist political economy consist almost entirely of a collection of policies or laws and definitions.

Third, in China's universities and post-secondary vocational colleges, like those in the Soviet Union, there are only colleges and departments specializing in commerce of consumer goods, but not in circulation of producer goods. Circulation of producer goods is called "material resources provision." It appears as a specialty within the planning department. Also, whether it is commerce of consumer goods, or "material resources provision," it is regarded as "sectoral economics" and not as political economy. It is studied as a problem in the direct exchange process, and not treated as an independent economic process that is independent of production but yet inseparable from it. In other words, it is studied within the scope of the second chapter, part 1, volume 1, of Marx's Capital, and not within the scope of the whole volume 2 of Capital. And it is not studied as a process of constant replenishment of the fund for producer goods and the fund for consumer goods in the social reproduction process.

In China, it seems that there are no papers or monographs that explicitly advocate the "natural economy viewpoint" or the "nonexistence of circulation process." But this does not show a lack of influence of this viewpoint among economists. On the contrary, there is a tacit acceptance of its dominant position. That is why the question of whether circulation exists in the socialist society has never been raised before.

Therefore, before we engage ourselves in concrete study of socialist circulation, let us first talk about whether "circulation" exists and what circulation is. In other words, it is necessary to talk about "circulation in general" without first considering the "concrete" social forms "circulation" assumes. Marx said: "Production in general is an abstraction, but a sensible abstraction in so far as it actually emphasizes and defines the common aspects and thus avoids repetition."[7] In this sense, it is reasonable and necessary to raise questions on "circulation in general" before we study the specific forms of circulation under socialist public ownership.

2. THE OBJECTIVE BASIS FOR THE EMERGENCE OF THE "NATURAL ECONOMY VIEWPOINT" AND THE "NONEXISTENCE OF CIRCULATION"

The negation of the socialist circulation process is not merely a result of subjective judgment. Nor is it merely a result of the influence of foreign economic thought. There are at least two objective reasons for the emergence of the "natural economy viewpoint" in socialist political economy.

First, the disappearance of private property and the consequent disappearance of commodity exchange in the blind and spontaneous market give people an illusion. People think that at least as far as the internal production relationship of the whole people ownership system is concerned, the difference between division of labor in society and technical division of labor within a plant alluded to in Marx's Capital, volume 1, part 4, chapter 12, has disappeared. The whole society (at least within the whole people ownership economy) has become a unified plant. And division of labor in society is identical to technical division of labor within a plant.[8] Therefore, circulation as a link among the various units in societal division of labor and its role as a medium no longer exists.

But this presents a serious misunderstanding of Marx's position. The transformation of private ownership into whole people ownership cannot entirely eliminate the differences between division of labor in society and technical division of labor within a plant. Similarly, the disappearance of the commodity exchange relationship cannot entirely eliminate exchange of products, and cannot eliminate circulation as an independent economic process. Division of labor in society, as distinct from technical division of labor within a plant, will still exist even in the production relationship within whole people ownership and even in the highest stage of communism.

Within the whole people ownership system and in the highest stage of communism, the difference between technical division of labor within a plant and division of labor in society is still not like what Adam Smith envisioned. That is, the observer in a plant can see with one glance all the numerous operations being performed on one spot, while in societal division of labor the spreading out of the work over great areas, and the great number of people employed in each branch of labor, obscures the connection. The difference between the two lies in this: technical division of labor occurs within an independent accounting unit and arises from exchange of different live labor. On the other hand, societal division of labor occurs among various independent accounting units and is realized through exchange of products.

The scope of direct exchange of labor cannot be very wide, and economic returns are calculated primarily through quotas. Consequently, economic comparison is limited in scope. Within the whole people ownership economy and in the future communist society, the more production is developed, the more detailed is societal division of labor and the closer is the coordination among financially independent enterprises. This division of labor can only be coordinated through exchange of products. And only through this can economic accounting be properly done and can social productiveness of labor be improved.

Second, as division of labor in society and technical division of labor converge in some significant respects, and as output of producer goods (even though the growth rate is quite high) always lags behind the planned needs for socialist construction, exchange of products (provision of material resources and technical equipments) among different sectors, and among millions of enterprises, must be conducted in the form of "distribution" or allocation. Therefore, it gives people a false impression that as far as the production relation within the whole people ownership economy is concerned, social production includes only production, distribution, and consumption. And circulation disappears because there is no need for it, or it is replaced by "distribution." In fact, the present form of providing material resources and technical equipment widely adopted in socialist countries is not "distribution" in the sense used in political economy. Instead, it is "rationing." It is a remedial measure under scarcity. It is certainly not a normal form of product exchange and product circulation built upon division of labor in society.

Therefore, in order to study the circulation process, and in order to explain the objective existence of the circulation process, it is first necessary to distinguish between the two entirely different categories of "distribution" and "exchange" in political economy.

Distribution refers first to the distribution of product (product value). If we exclude product (product value) that offsets material consumption, then distribution refers to the distribution of net product (net product value), namely, the distribution of necessary product for the subsistence of producers and their family dependents and the distribution of surplus product. It is the distribution of "v" and "m."[a] Marx pointed out that in any social production, distribution can be boiled down to the above-mentioned common characteristics once the different forms of distribution are abstracted from.[9]

But before distribution becomes distribution of products, it is (1) distribution of the means of production; and (2) (which is another aspect of the same situation) distribution of the members of society among the various types of production (the subsuming of the individuals under definite relations of production). It is evident that the distribution of products is merely a result of this distribution, which is comprised in the production process and determines the structure of production. To examine production divorced from this distribution which is a constituent part of it, is obviously idle abstraction, whereas conversely the distribution of products is automatically determined by that distribution which is initially a factor of production.[10]

Exchange is the transfer of products to consumers within the limit of distributed value to realize consumption. Marx said:

...a product becomes a real product only through consumption. For example, a dress is really a dress only by being worn, a house which is uninhabited is indeed not really a house; in other words a product as distinct from a simple natural object manifests itself as a product, becomes a product, only in consumption. It is only consumption which, by destroying the product, gives it the finishing touch, for the product is a product, not because it is materialized activity, but only in so far as it is an object for the active subject.[11]

In this sense, exchange is "an intermediate phase between production, distribution, which is determined by production, and consumption."[12]

Since exchange realizes or finally completes production and distribution, and circulation is exchange in general, then we can say that production and distribution are finally completed through the circulation process.

---

a) v is necessary labor product, i.e., product produced by laborers needed to guarantee the basic subsistence of their own and their family dependents. It is also called variable capital and is equivalent to wages. m is surplus labor product, i.e., product produced by laborers over and above v. It is more commonly denoted by s. See also Chapter 6 in this volume, pp. 113-15 — K.K.F.

From the above analysis of the two categories of "distribution" and "exchange," we can see that material resources provision is definitely not part of distribution. Rather, it is exchange or circulation itself. For under normal circumstances, the question of distributing necessary product and surplus product is not involved here. Nor is it a question of redistributing surplus product (product that is produced by laborers for society over and above that needed for the basic subsistence of their own and their family dependents). Here, material resources provision satisfies two purposes: one is the periodic replenishment of producer goods (fixed assets and raw materials) that have already been distributed but are consumed in the production process; another is the provision of needed construction materials and technical equipment equal to the capital fund that has already been distributed (or more correctly, redistributed) according to the state investment plan to expand production. This is precisely the question of exchange between the first and second categories[b] of social production and among various sectors and enterprises based on division of labor in society.

Of course, under normal circumstances, namely when material resources provision cannot satisfy the planned needs for production and construction, production fund that has already been distributed may be redistributed. When there is shortage of producer goods, producer goods that have been consumed in the production process cannot be replenished in time, and needed material resources for approved construction projects are not available on schedule. This amounts to a withdrawal of committed production funds or a change in the investment plan for which funds have already been appropriated. But this is obviously an abnormal situation involving a dislocation between material resources provision and construction plan. It is not the appropriate function of material resources provision.

Although we sometimes refer to material resources provision as the distribution of materials and technical equipment, material resources provision should in fact be carried out according to objective laws governing the socialist circulation process, and should not be treated as distribution in the sense used in political economy.

---

b) The first category of social production consists of producer goods, and the second category consists of consumer goods. — K.K.F.

3. TO UNDERSTAND THOROUGHLY THE CIRCULATION PROCESS WITHIN THE SOCIALIST WHOLE PEOPLE OWNERSHIP SYSTEM, IT IS NECESSARY TO APPRECIATE THE TWO FACTORS OF A PRODUCT AND THE TWO-FOLD CHARACTER OF LABOR

Marx said:

> In so far as exchange is a process, by which commodities are transferred from hands in which they are non-use-values, to hands in which they become use-values, it is a social circulation of matter. The product of one form of useful labor replaces that of another.[13]

From the viewpoint of the production relations within the socialist whole people ownership system, and even from the viewpoint of the highest stage of future communism, products are no longer commodities. Or, we can say the commodity and money relations have withered away. But, the above quoted passage from Marx is still appropriate if the term "commodities" is replaced by the term "products."

For example, a steel enterprise (or the whole steel sector) in the present or the future communist society must in its constant process of production and circulation supply its products to all other enterprises (or sectors), on the one hand, as its own products have no use value for itself (aside from the small amount of steel used by its affiliated repair shop and metal processing plant). On the other hand, it must constantly obtain through the circulation process from other independent accounting enterprises (or production sectors) various products to replenish equipment and raw materials that have been consumed. At the same time, its staff and workers must also constantly obtain basic consumer goods from the agricultural and light industrial sectors. This is the ever necessary continuous exchange "process" for products, or what Marx referred to as "social material replenishment," i.e., "the product of one form of useful labor replaces that of another."

Without this exchange of different labor products, the existence of the two major categories of social production, of the various sectors, and of millions and millions of enterprises would have been impossible. But since the millions and millions of enterprises involved in exchange are all independent accounting enterprises, their exchange of products must be exchange of equal values (aside from that part that must be delivered to the state or society and the state again allocates to enterprises in the form of investment). The principle governing the exchange of equal values with different use values must still be observed as an objective law. The only difference is that commodities in the capitalist society are exchanged through market competition in a blind and spontaneous manner. But here exchange is carried out consciously according to plan. Without such exchange, there can be no circulation process, and there can be no social reproduction. This is why we have repeatedly emphasized the two factors of a product and the two-fold character of labor in our discussion on the production process.

The paper by A. Ke-liu-qie-fu cited earlier is the only paper that I know of that treats exchange in the socialist society as an economic process. The author made many insightful comments on the content of the circulation process in this paper. But he dared not thoroughly reject the "natural economy viewpoint" in socialist political economy. And he did not accept the existence of the two factors of products and the two-fold character of labor. Therefore his arguments became contradictory in many instances. For example, he admitted on the one hand that the disappearance of commodity exchange did not lead to disappearance of exchange in general, and that exchange and circulation would exist forever just as production would. But he also said, "With the disappearance of commodity production, there is no need for exchange of equal values and consequently no need for commodity exchange." If products are not exchanged at equal values, i.e., the products that are obtained through exchange can have a higher or lower value than the products that are given up, then each incident of exchange amounts to a redistribution of enterprise capital fund. Isn't this exactly what the author of this paper objects to, i.e., treating material resources provision as distribution? Also, how can this kind of exchange promote economic accounting in enterprises? It seems that the author thinks that economic accounting is no longer necessary for enterprises in the future communist society. For the author says,

> In the completely communist system, the separation of production enterprises into individual economic units can be overcome. But it goes without saying that under the communist system some production units at the basic levels will be individual economic units relative to the whole society.

Are there still individual economic units or not? What is the difference between some basic level production units and individual economic units? Does the difference lie in whether economic accounting is required, or not? But how can a production unit without economic accounting improve its labor productivity if only records of inflow and outflow of products with concrete use values are kept and no comparison is made on the basis of uniform abstract labor? Here the author leaves us with a whole series of confused ideas.

4. SOCIALIST POLITICAL ECONOMY MUST STUDY CONCRETE PROBLEMS IN THE EXCHANGE PROCESS ITSELF

Marx devoted all of volume 2 of his Capital to the study of the capitalist circulation process. In volume 3 of Capital, Marx was still studying capitalist production by looking at "production and circulation as parts of an integral process." But whether it was in volume 2 or volume 3 of Capital, Marx always treated circulation as a process. Or as Marx put it, circulation was studied as part of the whole process of material replenishment in society. Exchange itself is perhaps what Marx referred to as "the two phases of the circulation process proper."[14] And Marx studied it in volume 1 of Capital when he dealt with the direct production process, when commodities and money were discussed. After he dealt with commodities in chapter 1, volume 1, of Capital, Marx studied the exchange process in chapter 2. This chapter has only twelve pages, being the shortest chapter in Capital. And in it Marx studied only the most basic relations in commodity exchange. Marx never studied in detail the concrete problems in the process of commodity exchange, such as the organization and channels of circulation. The reason is obvious. Marx's task was to reveal the essence hidden behind the spontaneous market circulation relation, and not to study how to organize this circulation. Furthermore, the characteristic of capitalism lies exactly in the fact that all things within the scope of circulation are carried on "spontaneously," without any need for organization and planning. As to the organization of capitalist commerce, it was the business of the capitalist to worry, and not the subject matter of Marx's Capital.

But socialist political economy should not be concerned merely with revealing the general laws of the circulation process. It must also be concerned with the detailed study of concrete problems such as the organization and channels of circulation. To start with, there should be a difference between our task of studying capitalist political economy as the proletariat – the gravediggers of the capitalist mode of production – and our task of studying socialist political economy as builders of the new society and as power-holders who organize the new economic system. Another more important reason is that the capitalist circulation process is spontaneous and blind, but the circulation process under the socialist planned economy is consciously organized. This essential difference overshadows the fact that the capitalist circulation process reflects an exploitive relation, while such a relation is absent in the socialist circulation process. If our task in the scientific study of a spontaneous circulation process is to reveal the objective laws of such a process, then our task in the scientific study of a consciously planned process is not only to reveal the objective laws according to which this planned process is organized, but also to find out how to build a perfect organization or management system according to these objective laws.

It seems that there is a widespread perception that the problem of building a management system for a socialist planned economy is a problem in the direct production process. We now know that this perception may not be correct. It is not a problem in the direct production process. Rather, it is a problem in the circulation process.

To say that it is a problem in the circulation process means that we can also say that it is a problem in the reproduction process. For as Marx said, circulation was a medium for reproduction. Also, if we look at the production process as a whole and as part of the reproduction process, production is part of the integral production and circulation process. But in this integral process, the key to building a planned economy lies primarily in the circulation process.

This is so because revolution in the direct production process was basically completed once the economy was nationalized and the exploitive class was eliminated. Revolution in the ownership system was the precondition for building a planned economy. Without this revolution, there could not have been a planned economy. Our present problems in the direct production process are the remedial tasks that need to be undertaken with the two revolutions. One is the remedial task involving the socialist revolution, for our socialist enterprise management system, newly built after the socialist revolution in ownership has been completed, and after exploitation has been eliminated, cannot be perfected right away. There are two reasons for this. One is the lack of experience; the other is the still existing remnants of old thinking. In short, revolution in the superstructure has not caught up with reform in the ownership system. But no matter how long this ideological class struggle is going to last, it is still a remedial task that needs to be done. Another remedial task involves the industrial revolution, or we can say the bourgeois revolution. Because old China was a backward country, and many of its big enterprises were managed by foreigners, we lacked experience in managing modern enterprises to start with. It was exactly in this sense that Lenin instructed the Russian working class after the October Revolution:

> The Taylor system, the last word of capitalism in this respect, like all capitalist progress, is a combination of the refined brutality of bourgeois exploitation and a number of the greatest scientific achievements in the field of analyzing mechanical motions during work, the elimination of superfluous and awkward motions, the elaboration of correct methods of work, the introduction of the best system of accounting and control, etc.[15]

But the problem of the circulation process is not merely a question of remedial work. Like the direct production process, revolution in the ownership system is completed in the circulation process. But as was said earlier, revolution in the ownership system is only a precondition for building a management system for the socialist planned economy, and not planned management itself. Also, as far as the direct production process itself is concerned, technical division of labor within the capitalist enterprise is built originally on the basis of a conscious and planned management system. When we say that we are replacing the blindness and spontaneity of chaotic market competition with the management system of a planned economy, our original meaning is not the direct production process within enterprises, but within the whole society, what Marx alluded to as the material replenishment process among millions of enterprises, namely, the circulation process. In this sense, the management system of the planned economy can only be said to be in the process of being established. And owing to the influence of the natural economy viewpoint in the past fifty years, socialist political economy has regarded this material replenishment process in society only as a matter of distribution, but not as a circulation process. Therefore, little study has been done on the objective laws governing the socialist circulation process.

There has been even less study on the management system or organization of planned circulation.

Therefore, in our lectures, we can only talk about a rough outline of the circulation process. We cannot even claim that we have studied the problem; all we can do is raise questions (and hope that these are roughly the right questions). Therefore, I only plan to spend five lectures on the circulation process. The first lecture is an introduction to circulation, the second lecture deals with the turnover and management of fixed capital fund, and the third lecture deals with the turnover and management of circulating capital fund. These first three lectures deal with general laws governing the socialist circulation process. In addition, the fourth lecture deals with the "supply and marketing of producer goods among state enterprises (exchange of products within the whole people ownership system)." And the fifth lecture deals with "socialist commerce (exchange of commodities among different ownership systems in the socialist society)." In the latter two lectures, the hope is expressed that some study will be done on concrete modes of organization and channels of socialist circulation. Exchange of products within the whole people ownership system and supply and marketing of producer goods among state enterprises are the leading mode of socialist circulation. They represent a microcosm of circulation organization in the future communist society. Exchange of commodities among different ownership systems or socialist commerce is a traditional form of the circulation process in the present stage of socialism. But however big the circulation volume of commodities is in the socialist society, it is always under the leadership of the whole people ownership production relation. If we do not first understand the circulation relation within the whole people ownership system, it is impossible for us to understand the leadership relation that state commerce has with cooperative commerce and farmers' markets.

5. THE STRUGGLE BETWEEN THE TWO LINES ON THE QUESTION OF CIRCULATION

There is now, to me, an incorrect economic view on circulation which attempts to explain and guide the socialist planned economy with the law of exchange value and the law of market competition by introducing the commodity-money relation into the internal relation of the whole people ownership system. This is the theoretical basis of the so-called economic "liberalization." But to oppose such a theory of commodity-money relation requires that the "natural economy viewpoint" also be opposed at the same time. In fact, the two are much like twins. The founders of the natural economy viewpoint were such old revisionists as Kautsky and Bukharin. And now those who attempt to introduce the commodity-money relation into the internal relation of the whole people ownership system and promote the policy of "liberalization" also often think that the future communist society will still be a natural economy without any circulation process.

April 1963

NOTES

1. This is part of my lecture notes used in my class at the Economics Department of the People's University of China.

2. Marx, Capital, volume 1, People's Publishing Company, 1975, p. 390. [English translation based on the English edition published by Progress Publishers, Moscow, 1954, volume 1, p. 332 — K.K.F.]

3. Marx, A Contribution to the Critique of Political Economy, People's Publishing Company, 1976, p. 208. [English translation based on the English edition published by Progress Publishers, Moscow, 1970, p. 204 — K.K.F.]

4. Ibid., p. 81 [Moscow English edition, pp. 98-99 — K.K.F.].

5. Engels, Anti-Duhring, People's Publishing Company, 1974, p. 291. [English translation based on Chinese translation — K.K.F.]

6. A. Ke-liu-qie-fu, Scholarly Papers, volume 18, Leningrad, Engels Soviet Business College, 1961. [English translation based on Sun's Chinese translation — K.K.F.]

7. Marx, A Contribution to the Critique of Political Economy, People's Publishing Company, 1976, p. 195. [English translation based on the English edition published by Progress Publishers, Moscow, 1970, p. 190 — K.K.F.]

8. Marx pointed out in Capital, volume 1, part 4, chapter 12, that there were six differences between division of labor in society and detail operations in a workshop: (1) Products from the constituent units in societal labor division are commodities. But detail laborers in a workshop produce no commodities. It is only the common product of all the detail laborers that becomes a commodity. (2) Division of labor in society is brought about by the purchase and sale of the products of different branches of industry, while the connection between the detail operations in a workshop is based on the sale of the labor power of several workmen to one capitalist. (3) Division of labor in the workshop implies concentration of production in the hands of one capitalist; the division of labor in society implies their dispersion among many independent producers of commodities. (4) While within the workshop the iron law of proportionality subjects definite numbers of workmen to definite functions, in the society outside the workshop, chance and caprice have full play in distributing the producers and their means of production among the various

branches of industry. (5) The a priori system of proportions, on which the division of labor within the workshop is regularly carried out, becomes in the division of labor within the society an a posterior, nature-imposed necessity, controlling the lawless caprice of the producers, and perceptible in the barometrical fluctuations of market prices. (6) Division of labor within the workshop implies the undisputed authority of the capitalist over men, that are but parts of a mechanism that belongs to him. Division of labor within society brings into contact independent commodity producers, who acknowledge no other authority but that of competition, of coercion exerted by the pressure of flimsy mutual interest. Marx pointed out that the same bourgeois mind that praises division of labor in the workshop, lifelong annexation of the laborer to a partial operation, and his complete subjection to capital as being an organization of labor that increases its productiveness, is the same bourgeois mind that denounces with equal vigor every conscious attempt to socially control and regulate the process of production, as an inroad upon such sacred things as property rights, freedom, and unrestricted play for the bent of the individual capitalist. It is very characteristic that the enthusiastic apologists of the factory system have nothing more damning to urge against a general organization of the labor of society than that it would turn all society into one immense factory (Capital, People's Publishing Company, 1975, volume 1, pp. 389-95). [English translation based on the English edition published by Progress Publishers, Moscow, 1954, volume 1, pp. 335-37 – K.K.F.]

9. Marx, Capital, volume 3, People's Publishing Company, 1975, p. 993. [Moscow English edition, volume 3, 1959, p. 878 – K.K.F.]

10. Marx, A Contribution to the Critique of Political Economy, People's Publishing Company, 1976, p. 206. [English translation based on the English edition published by Progress Publishers, Moscow, 1970, pp. 201-02 – K.K.F.]

11. Ibid., p. 201 [Moscow English edition, p. 196 – K.K.F.].

12. Ibid., p. 208 [Moscow English edition, p. 204 – K.K.F.].

13. Marx, Capital, volume 1, People's Publishing Company, 1975, p. 122. [English translation based on the English edition published by Progress Publishers, Moscow, 1954, volume 1, p. 106 – K.K.F.]

14. Marx, Capital, volume 2, People's Publishing Company, 1975, p. 389. [English translation based on the English edition published by Progress Publishers, Moscow, 1956, volume 2, p. 355 – K.K.F.]

15. Lenin, "The Immediate Tasks of the Soviet Government," Complete Works of Lenin, volume 27, p. 237. [English translation based on the English edition of Selected Works of Lenin, volume 2, published by Progress Publishers, Moscow, 1975, p. 603 – K.K.F.]

6

Pursue Socialist Profit with Confidence

In their disastrous attempt to subvert the proletarian dictatorship and restore capitalism, the Wang [Hongwen] , Zhang [Chunqiao] , Jiang [Qing] , and Yao [Wenyuan] "Gang of Four" deliberately distorted the policy of economic accounting in socialist enterprises for greater profit to the state as "profit in command" and "a preparation for capitalist restoration." They peddled the reactionary fallacy that "profit is condemnable and loss is justified," as if profit were capitalism and loss were socialism. Under the sabotage of the "Gang of Four," everybody was afraid to mention profit. They felt guilty whenever they mentioned profit. As far back as the late 1950s and the early 1960s, Chen Boda, the political swindler, schemer, and ambitious climber, teamed up with Zhang Chunqiao the Nationalist agent, to fan up a "communist fever." They denied the legitimate roles played by commodities, money, and the law of value in the socialist period. They opposed the principle of distribution according to labor; and under the pretext of opposing "profit in command," they vilified profit sent to the state by socialist enterprises. That was a difficult time for financial cadres in enterprises. One finance section chief in an advanced enterprise in Shanghai told me: "The task of fulfilling the profit quota sent to the state is a rigid one. We cannot be short for even a copper coin. Yet we are not supposed to talk about the task at all." I was surprised to hear that. Could it be that there was something wrong in fulfilling a state task? Under this circumstance, some enterprises suffered a reduction in profit. Quite a few suffered losses. Some of these had to depend on permanent state subsidies. These abnormal conditions worsened considerably in the heyday of the "four scourges."[a] On the eve of their downfall, the "Gang of Four" had

a) "Four scourges" here refers to the Wang, Zhang, Jiang, and Yao "Gang of Four." — K.K.F.

pushed the national economy to the brink of collapse. But they were still not satisfied and kept on complaining that "profit in command" had not been thoroughly criticized. What a joke!

From a theoretical viewpoint, their vilification of profit in socialist enterprises, like their denial of the existence of commodities, money, value, and distribution according to labor in socialist society, reflected their nostalgia for a feudalistic, self-sufficient natural economy. This idea of a natural economy belonged to Chen Boda and was criticized by Chairman Mao as early as 1959.

From a political viewpoint, this propogation of their idea was intended to serve their purpose of usurping the Party and seizing power by misleading the people, sabotaging the national economy, and shifting blame onto other people. In our struggle to expose and criticize the "Gang of Four," we must distinguish the correct line from the incorrect line, the correct thought from the incorrect thought, and the correct theory from the incorrect theory. We must expose their intrigue and mobilize the masses to pursue socialist enterprise profit with confidence.

In 1963 I wrote an internal research report entitled "The Profit Target in the Management System of the Socialist Planned Economy"[b] (hereafter abbreviated as the Profit Report) to attack this reactionary idea of a natural economy championed by Chen Boda, Zhang Chunqiao, and others. The theme of that report was that socialist enterprise profit should be distinguished from capitalist enterprise profit; it was wrong to treat socialist enterprise profit as if it were capitalist enterprise profit; and the reputation of socialist profit should be restored by reducing loss and increasing profit. That report was eagerly seized upon by Chen Boda and the "Gang of Four." It was used as a living model of "profit in command" and criticized three times in the national press. In the heyday of Chen Boda and the "Gang of Four," I was deprived of my right to speak. I was thus unable to defend my ideas. The academic circle was naturally unable to conduct a reasoned debate on the topic. Today, Chen Boda and the "Gang of Four" have been dumped on the garbage heap of history, and the Party once again calls on us to reduce loss and increase profit. Although there are inadequacies and mistakes in that Profit Report, the basic idea of the report is still

b) This report was included in the Chinese edition of Sun Yefang's <u>Shehuizhuyi jingji de ruogan lilun wenti</u> [Some Theoretical Issues in Socialist Economics] but, to avoid excessive content duplication, is not included in this volume. – K.K.F.

sound. (The mistake relates to the question of bonus. See the last section of this paper for a discussion of this point.) In our present concern to put the country in order, the existence and size of profit in enterprises are important issues. It is therefore entirely necessary to explain clearly from a theoretical viewpoint the issues relating to socialist profit.

1. WHAT IS PROFIT?

For the sake of clarification, let us first discuss what profit in the socialist economy is, and what role it should play in the management system of the socialist planned economy.

Profit is a component of the material wealth produced by the staff and workers in the material production department. The wealth produced by the staff and workers of the production department can be divided into three components: the first component offsets the material consumption in the production process, i.e., the consumption of fixed assets and raw materials. It is equivalent to Marx's constant capital (c) in his Capital. The second component consists of wage compensation to staff and workers. It is the consumer goods distributed by society to the staff and workers and their dependents. It is equivalent to Marx's variable capital (v). The above two components comprise what is generally known as costs. The third component is the surplus value, and is equivalent to Marx's m. In the capitalist system, profit is the modified form of surplus value. Stalin thought that the second component of the material wealth produced by the staff and workers of socialist enterprises, namely the wage component (v), should be called product produced by the workers "for themselves," and that the third component, namely the surplus value (m), should be called product produced "for society." This idea of Stalin's is very correct! In the socialist society, therefore, profit is a monetized product value produced by the staff and workers of the production department for society. Now let us analyze how, in the socialist society, we should treat these three components (c, v, m) of the total social product.

Let us start with c. As was said above, this c stands for consumption of fixed assets and raw materials. With the advance of modern science and technology, the value of fixed assets, namely machines and equipment, is increasing. The increase in productivity also increases the consumption of raw materials. This is then the objective tendency referred to by Marx as the ever-increasing organic composition of capital.[c] But our subjective efforts must still be to reduce c through increasing production and reducing material consumption.

Next, let us look at the second component, i.e., the wage component, of the product value. With improvement in productivity, the standard of living of the people in the socialist society, including the standard of living of the staff and workers in the material production department, should be continually raised. First, however, raising the standard of living of the staff and workers in the material production department indicates merely that the material quantity of consumption has increased. The value of this component of the product need not increase. Therefore, the relative weight of v in the newly produced value of v + m need not increase. Instead, we should try to keep it down. Second, the rise in people's standard of living does not consist solely of development in such material production departments as industry, agriculture, communications, and transportation. It should also be reflected in the increase of employment in service industries such as science, culture, education, health, and other production activities divorced from material production and the general rise of the standard of living for the staff and workers in these industries. The increasing proportion of employment in activities divorced from material production (the broadly defined service industries) in the employed labor force is an important indicator of high social productive forces and affluence. Yet these personnel who are divorced from material production must be supported by consumer goods produced by the staff and workers in the material production department. In other words, they depend on the m component of the product value, or the monetized profit, for their living. This is to say that the first component (c) and the second component (v) should be reduced. Only when this is accomplished can the third component (m) be increased. To further develop productive forces and to further expand reproduction, it is also necessary to increase accumulation. And accumulation also comes from the third component of m. Therefore, improvement in productivity and a general rise in people's standard of living imply a relative reduction in the share of production "for themselves" in the total social product by the staff and workers in the material production department, that is, a relative reduction in the v component. At the same time, they imply a

c) The organic composition of capital is generally defined as C/v. For details, see Editor's Introduction, Table 1. — K.K.F.

corresponding increase in the share of production "for society" in the total social product (namely, m) by the staff and workers in material production.

In addition, in the socialist society there are two ways of improving the staff and workers' standard of living — increasing wages and reducing product prices. And these two means are under the unified control of our government and not determined by individual enterprises. So far as individual enterprises are concerned, they should raise labor productivity by improving operation and management and updating technology. The aim is to reduce relatively or absolutely the consumption of live labor, to reduce the share of v.

In general, whether it is the social product or the total enterprise product, the c and v components (generally known as costs) should be as low as possible. With lower costs, the share of profit sent to the state will increase. In other words, the share of labor and product for society contributed by the enterprise staff and workers increases. Therefore, when we agree that it is better to reduce costs, we should agree that it is better to have higher enterprise profit. Under constant prices, reducing costs is synonymous with increasing profit. If it is all right to mention cost reduction, it is meaningless to taboo the mention of profit increase. We should pursue socialist enterprise profit with confidence. The success of enterprise management should be judged on how much costs (c and v) can be reduced, how much profit sent to the state is increased, and how much the share of labor and product for society (m) is raised.

But in the eyes of Chen Boda and the "Gang of Four," it was a crime for socialist enterprises to reduce costs and increase the share of product for society and profit. Ironically, their livelihood depended on just this profit produced by the staff and workers of the material production department. In addition to their official wages, they also misappropriated public money for their own use. Wang Hongwen spent more than 20,000 yuan of public fund when he lived in Shanghai for three months. Jiang Qing spent a large sum of public fund on Jiang Qing-style garments as gifts to her friends. All these monies came from the profit sent to the state by enterprises. In the past, feudal bureaucrats and scholars avoided mentioning money directly to show that money matters were beneath their "dignity." But this was no more than a case of hypocrisy. Now Chen Boda and the "Gang of Four's" attempt to vilify enterprise profit was much more sinister in intent. They wanted to corrupt people's minds, confuse their thinking, and sabotage the national economy. With the economy in shambles, they could then blame others to fulfill their desire to usurp the Party and seize power.

2. "A CERTAIN AMOUNT OF PROFIT"

Because of the persistent threat of being accused of favoring "profit in command" posed by Chen Boda and the "Gang of Four," few people dared to violate the verbal taboo on "profit." Consequently, enterprise finance became "illegitimate activities" which could "only be done but not talked about." Those who were engaged in theoretical work were equally intimidated. They dared not defend "profit" with confidence. But this was too important a task to be put aside. Sometimes, it was necessary to talk about "profit," or even to defend "socialist enterprise profit." Therefore, for a long period of time, statements like the following were typical: it is bad to have "profit in command" or pursue "profit at all costs." But it is all right to go after "a certain amount of profit," or "reasonable profit." What is "a certain amount of profit" or "reasonable profit"? Does it refer to the quantity or the nature of the profit? If it refers to the quantity of profit, does it mean 10 percent, 20 percent, 30 percent, or some other percentage? To propose "a certain amount of profit" is clearly hedging.

Suppose the average profit rate is 20 percent in a certain industry. This 20 percent is then the contribution of labor and product for society by the staff and workers of this industry. Does it mean that the staff and workers of each enterprise or the whole industry should not try to increase their contribution of product for society and profit to the state by improving operating and management, updating technology, raising labor productivity, and reducing costs? Does it mean that they should be satisfied with a "happy medium" of a 20 percent profit rate?

For the country as a whole, profit sent to the state from state enterprises is a major source of government revenues. Does it mean that our finance departments should be satisfied with "a certain amount of profit"? and we should not require enterprises to increase their share of profit sent to the state while increasing production to improve the whole people's standard of living? Does it mean that we should allow government revenues to stay at the same level forever? I think most people would agree that given the above conditions, profit sent to the state and hence this source of government revenues should be as high as possible and not as low as possible.

Such phrases as "a certain amount of profit" or "reasonable profit" are not only unclear in meaning, they are actually harmful in practice. In my 1963 Profit Report I wrote:

> We cannot say quantitatively that an enterprise is socialist if its profit rate does not exceed "a certain" percentage a year or it is revisionist or capitalist if its profit rate exceeds a certain percentage. Under the Party's call to "reduce loss and increase profit," those enterprises suffering from loss are now anxious to eliminate loss. But as soon as they make "a certain" amount of profit, they relax their efforts. This then is a concrete reflection of the idea of "a certain amount of profit."

3. A CONFUSION OF CONCEPTS

Because of the constant threat of being accused of favoring "profit in command" posed by Chen Boda and the "Gang of Four," "profit" became a "prohibited area" for many theoretical and practical workers. They dared not mention "increasing profit." Instead, they only talked about "reducing costs." They dared not say it was better to have higher profit. Instead, they went after "a certain amount of profit." Recently, a new way of avoiding the direct mention of "profit" has appeared. That is, "profit" is transformed into "accumulation." Instead of directly calling on enterprises to increase profit sent to the state, they are called on to increase accumulation for the state. This is another confusion in concepts. Just as was said above, profit is the complement of costs. Reducing costs is equivalent to increasing profit. Or, to increase profit, costs must be reduced. Similarly, accumulation is the complement of consumption. With constant output and profit, to require the staff and workers to increase accumulation for the state is to mandate a reduction in people's standard of living. This runs counter to the socialist economic principle. It also violates socialist economic principles and Party and state policies. The purpose of calling profit by the name of accumulation is to avoid the "prohibited area" of "profit." However, this avoidance inadvertently turns into poor publicity for violating socialist economic principles and Party and state policies.

Some writers dare not directly say that it is glorious to try to increase profit delivered to the state. Instead, they say it is glorious to increase accumulation for the state. This statement appears to be harmless. But a careful examination reveals that it implies that it is not glorious for the profit delivered to the state, or government revenues, to be used for consumption. But it is no secret to anyone that most state revenues are used for consumption. That is to say, they are used for national defense, operating expenses of state government agencies, science, culture, education, health, and wages for personnel in the non-material production sectors. In short, most government revenues are used for the above-mentioned public and individual consumption. Only a small portion is used for accumulation. If only accumulation is glorious and consumption is not, then most of the profit delivered to the state by enterprise staff and workers is not glorious. This conceptual confusion is a result of avoiding the direct mention of profit and renaming it accumulation. It is another example of bad publicity.

4. THREE LINES OF DEMARCATION BETWEEN SOCIALIST ENTERPRISE PROFIT AND CAPITALIST PROFIT

This tendency to verbally avoid "profit," shying away from the "prohibited area" of "profit" and substituting the concepts of "a certain amount of profit" and "accumulation" for the concept of profit, actually dates back a long time. Therefore, in my 1963 Profit Report I suggested that we should not replace economics with semantics and that we should not vainly search for another term to replace "profit." Instead, we should fundamentally demarcate between socialist enterprise profit and capitalist enterprise profit.

In my 1963 Profit Report I suggested three lines of demarcation between socialist profit and capitalist profit. Even though Chen Boda and the "Gang of Four" treated this report of mine as a natural example of "profit in command" for criticism, they dared not touch upon these three lines of demarcation. I am quoting them in brief as follows:

"First, the class nature of profit is different. Capitalist profit represents capitalist exploitation of workers. But socialist enterprise profit is wealth produced by the staff and workers of production enterprises for expanded social reproduction and the public needs of society.

"Second, the ends and means of production are different. The end of capitalist production is to pursue profit for its own sake. Capitalist commodity production is merely a means to profit. The end of socialist production is to produce material wealth. But to achieve this end, it has to be good at improving labor productivity, reducing product costs, and increasing profit.

"Third, the method of obtaining profit is different. Under capitalism, profit is obtained through market competition, price fluctuation, speculation, and manipulation. Socialist profit is based on the implementation of centrally determined goals and policies, planned production, planned prices, and stable coordination between supply, production, and marketing. Speculation and manipulation are ruled out. Under these conditions, profit can be obtained only through diligent efforts in updating technology, improving operation and management, and reducing costs."

I think the above three lines of demarcation basically illustrate the essential distinctions between socialist enterprise profit and capitalist profit. Whether these lines of demarcation are exact can of course be discussed further. I hope that those who are engaged in theoretical research or practical work can criticize and correct them, that together we can come up with a few guidelines for those in socialist finance work and theoretical research to follow, so that we can pursue socialist enterprise profit with confidence and work toward increasing enterprise profit delivered to the state and government revenues.

So long as our enterprise operation follows the socialist guidelines, the resulting enterprise profit should be regarded as legitimate socialist enterprise profit and should be pursued with confidence. Such enterprise profit is good, and the more the better. But when the above guidelines are violated, for example, when an enterprise does not produce according to the state plan and pursues profit through speculation and manipulation, then the resulting profit is not socialist profit. And when such profit was stolen and wasted by Wang Hongwen and Jiang Qing, it simply means that the higher the profit, the greater the exploitation imposed on the people. In such cases, we should call on the staff and workers of the enterprises concerned to take back the power stolen by [the Gang] so that they can no longer exploit the blood and sweat of the working class.

Chen Boda, and the "Gang of Four" and company said that this Profit Report of mine advocated "profit in command" and "profit at all costs." I consider this a slander and an attempt to fabricate excuses for my political persecution.

5. ON THE BASIC ISSUE OF PRICE FORMATION

But in our history of socialist construction, there indeed have been incidents of capitalist pursuit of profit contrary to the overall interests of the state and the people. These pursuits can be characterized as: "do it if it is profitable, skip it if it is not profitable;

do more if it promises big profit, do less if it promises small profit." For example, in the early 1960s when there was an urgent need for agricultural machines in the communes and brigades, an agricultural machine plant ignored its state-assigned quotas of agricultural machines to produce small iron beds. The reason was that the prices of agricultural machines were fixed at too low a level with little or no profit at all. But the prices of beds were set high with big profits to be earned. Another widespread tendency in the machine-building industry was that plants liked to produce whole machines and disliked producing machine parts. The reason was that there was profit in whole machines and little profit in machine parts because too much labor was involved. These were examples often used by those who criticized "profit in command" and opposed the evaluation of enterprise performance according to the size of its profit. People usually blamed such tendencies on inadequate educational work, and on politics not being in command. True, such reasons were involved. But why must the prices of agricultural machines and iron beds, and those of whole machines and machine parts, be set in such a way that there were substantial profit differentials among them? If prices were set properly so that the differences in profit are eliminated and the material basis for overlooking the state plan in pursuit of profit is taken away, wouldn't educational work be more effective?

Since the support of agriculture is an important political task in the national economy, and since the labor costs of machine parts are high and a whole machine can be idled for the lack of a part, why then should prices be set in favor of beds and whole machines at the expense of agricultural machines and parts? The commonly offered explanation is this: agricultural machines are made in support of agriculture, and their prices should not be high; iron beds are a consumer good, and the consumer goods industry is a primary source of state "accumulation"; therefore their price can be set higher. Another explanation is this: under imperialist rule, if a machine was bought from a foreign country, machine parts always had to be bought from the same country. Therefore, imperialism used high prices for parts to oppress the colonial and semicolonial countries. Our socialist country must therefore reverse this tendency and deliberately set prices of parts lower, and so on.

In short, according to these explanations, product price determination is not based on economic laws, or values, but on subjective wishes. This is exactly the position taken by Si-te-lu-mi-lin, an old Russian economist, viz., there is no price policy unless prices deviate from values. But facts show that if policies are implemented by divorcing prices from values, the objective results often turn out to be opposite to subjective wishes. For example, the subjective wishes may be to emphasize the production of agricultural machines and parts, but the lower prices set turn their production into an unwelcome task. With the exception of tobacco, alcoholic drinks, and such special goods, the best price policy, in my view, is to set product prices according to their values (I argue below that product prices should be set according to their production prices; but this is not contradictory to the principle of setting prices according to values).

This is to say, prices should be set according to objective economic laws, not subjective wishes.

Two other problems arise when prices deviate from values: First, it does not facilitate economic accounting. When expensive things are treated as cheap and cheap things as expensive, there is no longer any objective standard for economic accounting. Second, the proportional relations among the various sectors of the national economy are distorted. In the early 1970s, an article written by Cai Zheng was published in Renmin ribao [People's Daily]. It dealt with the importance of agriculture in the national economy. The data showed that agriculture accounted for a little more than 10 percent of state revenues. About the same time, a New China News Agency dispatch reported that a production brigade increased its earnings by reducing costs through proper economic accounting. The conclusion of the release also stressed the importance of agriculture in the national economy because its contribution to state revenues amounted to a fraction above 10 percent. But as early as the late 1950s, Chairman Mao had already doubted the accuracy of this percentage figure. After carefully reviewing a draft plan for national economic construction, he raised a question for those in planning and statistics work: How is it possible that the contribution to state revenues from the 200 million whole and partial labor units in the rural areas amounts to only a fraction above 10 percent and the contribution from the mere 10 million staff and workers in industry and transportation amounts to more than 80 percent? The reason is that this account had been distorted by prices which deviated from values! Because prices of agricultural and sideline products were set low, the contribution to state revenues by peasants (including only public grain) computed at these prices amounted to only a fraction above 10 percent. But after more than ten years, the author of this article still used this percentage figure to show the importance of agriculture. This shows that when prices deviate from values, the proportional relations in the national economy are completely distorted. For lack of a better picture, we must then still use a distorted figure which indicates the small share of agriculture in the national economy to show the significance of agriculture.

Since Liberation, our government has raised the purchase prices for agricultural products several times. The purpose was to reduce or eliminate the price differentials between industrial and agricultural products left over from the rule of imperialism and the Nationalist Party. Some people, therefore, think that these price differentials no longer exist. Whoever talks about this problem must then be guilty of vilifying socialism and attacking the fiscal policy of the Party and the state. Now, the Party Central Committee led by Chairman Hua has raised the question of price adjustments. Chairman Hua [Guofeng], Vice-Chairman Deng [Xiaoping], and Vice-Chairman Li [Xiannian] separately raised the question of adjusting the relative prices between industrial and agricultural products in several speeches. This is a wise decision. This is a decisive economic measure which can promote agricultural production, especially food production. Because prices for food grain are low, production teams are not interested in increasing their production once they have produced enough to satisfy the food needs of their members and their tax and purchase quotas from the state. But they are extremely interested in other crops and sideline activities, especially transportation, which can increase their cash income. Therefore, for a long time, no matter how much emphasis was put on ideological and political education, and how much the tendencies of favoring sidelines to agriculture, leaving agriculture for commerce, and forsaking agriculture for transportation were criticized, there was very little improvement in the situation. The reason was that the economic measures were not appropriately adjusted and the problem of cash shortage for the members was never solved. If agriculture is the foundation of the national economy and food grain is its most precious treasure, is it reasonable that cash shortage should become a problem when one is engaged in agriculture and food production?

Now that the principle of adjusting the relative prices of industrial and agricultural products by raising the prices of agricultural products is agreed upon, there remains the problem of implementation. The problem of adjusting the prices of industrial and agricultural products is really the problem of raising the prices at which the state purchases agricultural products. According to one estimate, if the state must pay value-determined prices for the agricultural products it buys, the additional expenditure amounts to the annual investment figure for expanded reproduction. "Since wool must come from sheep," state revenues must ultimately come from industry (including communications and transportation) and agriculture. Therefore, it is not realistic or feasible to expect the price adjustments to be financed by the state treasury. This is because:

First, the state cannot do without the investment for socialist expanded reproduction.

Second, after the prices of industrial and agricultural products are adjusted according to their values, that part of the state revenues which comes from the purchase of agricultural products through the so-called "price lever" will no longer be available. This source of revenues is not presently indicated among state revenues because of the artificially low prices for agricultural products. Instead, state revenues from agriculture include only the agricultural tax known as public grain. That is why the contribution to state revenues from agriculture amounts to only a little more than 10 percent and the contribution from industry amounts to more than 80 percent. When this concealed source of revenues is gone, the contribution to national construction by the peasants is then confined to that of public grain. If the quantity of this public grain is unchanged, the share of state revenues represented by them (including public cotton and other direct agricultural taxes) will increase from a fraction above 10 percent to several percentage points above 10 percent. But it is also unreasonable that 80–90 percent of the total population in agriculture contributes only several percentage points above 10 percent of the state revenues and 10–20 percent of the total population in the urban areas (and only about half of them are directly engaged in material production) contributes more than 80 percent of the state revenues, for then the contribution of agriculture to national construction is too small.

6. THE FORM OF PEASANT BURDEN

In fact, as early as the late 1950s, Chairman Mao was already paying attention to this question. At that time, he proposed that the law of value should be respected and issued the directive that the principle of exchange at equal values between industrial and agricultural products should be observed. That is to say, Chairman Mao admitted that price differentials between industrial and agricultural products existed and that the problem must be solved. But why then has the problem not been solved? That is because the problem of finding an alternative source of revenues to finance the increased expenditure resulting from higher agricultural prices has not been completely resolved. What can we do now? How can we achieve the goal of raising prices of agricultural and sideline products and adjusting the relative prices of industrial and agricultural products suggested by Chairman Hua and the Party Central Committee? I think the solution lies not in reducing the proper state tax burden of the peasants (this does not refer to the illegal burden forced on the peasants in Xiang Xiang, Hunnan Province, as was recently reported in the press; this is contrary to the Party policy and must be stopped immediately), but in changing the form of the burden. Therefore, I think the following requirements must be fulfilled in the process of adjusting the relative prices of industrial and agricultural products and raising the purchase prices of agricultural products: (1) There should be no reduction in state revenues. (2) But neither should there be any increase in peasant burden. With the exception of increased burden on peasants imposed illegally by "local policy," there should not be any reduction in their contribution to the state. (3) There should be no adverse effects on the livelihood of the urban population.

Some people cannot help but wonder: if after the price adjustments there is no reduction in peasant burden and no increase in state revenues, isn't this an exercise in futility?

No, it is not an exercise in futility. It bears on the question of agricultural production, especially the question whether food production can be increased. I will elaborate this point below.

When the prices of agricultural products are too low, the price differentials between industrial and agricultural products represent a form of state burden on the peasants. But this burden is not overt and direct. It is indirect and is obtained as indirect tax through the so-called price lever. This is an inefficient method because the size of the burden is not fixed. The greater the amount of agricultural and sideline products sold to the state, the more this burden by the state increases. This is a form of burden which adversely affects the production enthusiasm of the peasants. If the contribution now obtained from the peasants through price differentials between industrial and agricultural products is converted into direct taxes (in the form of public grain, public cotton, etc.), but the absolute amount of the burden is strictly fixed by law for a number of years, then the peasants would be able to reap the whole value of the agricultural and sideline products sold to the state in excess of the fixed direct agricultural tax. And if the relative prices among various agricultural and sideline products are reasonable, then approximately equal benefits would be obtained no matter which of the twelve agricultural products ("grain, cotton, edible oil, hemp, silk, tea, sugar, vegetables, tobacco, fruit, medicinal herbs, and miscellaneous crops") are grown or which sideline products are produced. This way, the state-assigned tasks of planned cropping to suit local conditions can be implemented more easily and production enthusiasm can be increased. When agricultural production is increased, and the people become richer, state revenues will also increase. This is Chairman Mao's idea of storing wealth in the people. As to how the livelihood of urban population can be maintained, I think there are at least two solutions to be considered. The first one is to keep the retail prices of agricultural and sideline products (mainly food grain) unchanged; the losses resulting from the excess of purchase prices over selling prices will be subsidized by the treasury. The second one is to provide subsidies to the consumers according to the staff and workers' consumption quotas of food grain and the degree of the price increase. No matter which method is adopted, the government must increase its cash expenditure. But first, because the amount of material wealth provided by the peasants has not fallen, only the monetized value of this wealth is increased owing to the price increase; second, the physical quantity of consumer goods received by the workers has not increased; only the monetized value of these consumer goods is increased. And since these two increases are equal (because the two physical quantities and two value figures have not changed), the government can use the former increase to finance the latter increase.[d] This is exactly the maze

d) If there are no indirect taxes from agricultural products through the price lever, all agricultural products purchased by the state (over and above those delivered to the state as direct taxes in kind) to feed the non-peasants must be valued at the higher adjusted prices. The lost revenues to the state from this source must be offset by a higher delivery quota of agricultural products to the state as direct taxes in order to maintain the existing tax burden on the peasants. Otherwise, the treasury will have no revenues to finance created by the deviation of prices from values that makes some people hesitate before "major surgery" is undertaken to adjust the price differentials between industrial and agricultural products.

7. RESTORE THE REPUTATION OF "CAPITAL PROFIT RATE"

For a long time in the past, under the pretext of criticizing "profit in command," socialist enterprise profit suffered an undeserved stigma and was subjected to unjustified attacks and criticism. On careful examination, one can see that these attacks and criticisms came from three kinds of people.

The first kind maliciously attacked profit for ulterior motives because of their ambitions and intrigues. They were Lin Biao, Chen Boda, and the "Gang of Four" and company. I will not dwell on them here.

The second kind of people criticized so-called "profit in command" out of their concern and love for socialist finance work. But these comrades were unable to distinguish theoretically between socialist profit and capitalist profit. They were still affected by their disdain for money, characteristic of feudal scholars and gentlemen. My criticism of these comrades can be seen in the first few paragraphs of this paper.

The criticism of the third kind of people against so-called "profit in command" was directed against the capitalist method of operation characterized by "do it if it is profitable, skip it if it is not profitable; do more if it promises big profit, do less if it promises small profit." This method of operation should be criticized. But critics only looked at the problem in ideological and educational terms. They did not wonder why in a socialist society where all production departments are supposed to satisfy public needs and people's livelihood needs there are differences in profit among production departments and products, and why those production departments and

---

the price and/or wage subsidies given to the non-peasants. In the post-1978 adjustment period, treasury subsidies to cover the excess of purchasing prices over selling prices in agricultural products led to an ever larger budget deficit as output and state purchase of agricultural products increased. This occurred because direct taxes in kind were not increased enough to offset the higher prices paid to the peasants and consumption of agricultural products by non-peasants increased somewhat. See Xue Muqiao, Current Economic Problems in China, edited and translated by K. K. Fung (Boulder, Colorado: Westview Press, 1982), pp. 73-75, 84-85. — K.K.F.

products with little or no profit are often the ones that are regarded as important by society and leadership organs. Is it because the labor productivity of the staff and workers in these departments is particularly low so that their contribution of labor and product to society is particularly low? Certainly not. There is obviously only one explanation: The product prices are set incorrectly. In effect, unreasonable prices and prices divorced from values amount to redistribution of the national income. They transfer values created in the production process of one product to the account of another product. Because of this, we must talk about the theory of price formation when we talk about profit. When Chen Boda and the "Gang of Four" controlled the communication media, there was a strange idea that price policy was not a suitable research topic for economists. Rather it was a topic for propaganda. But how can propaganda be conducted without research?

Now that the Center has proposed raising the prices of agricultural and sideline products and adjusting the relative prices of industrial and agricultural products, economists should conduct in-depth research into this problem in coordination with practical workers so as to facilitate the implementation of this task proposed by the Party Central Committee and Comrade Hua Guofeng.

We think that prices should be set according to product values and oppose the principles of setting prices independent of values. But this is only a basic principle. And it does not mean that the price of every product must be absolutely equal to its value. If the price of every product were absolutely equal to its value, then the following would happen: Big and foreign enterprises make money, and small and indigenous enterprises lose money. But the profitability of big and foreign enterprises does not necessarily result from the subjective efforts of their staff and workers. And the unprofitability of small and indigenous enterprises does not necessarily result from inadequate subjective efforts of their staff and workers. There are objective conditions at work here. This is because the big and foreign enterprises have better equipment, bigger investment, and more advanced technology. These plus large scale production, high labor productivity, and low costs naturally lead to high profit. Conversely, the small and indigenous enterprises have poor equipment, low labor productivity, and high costs. As a result, not only do they not make money, they lose money. All this was determined by the investment plan and technical design when the plants were first built. They are therefore accomplished facts for the present staff and workers.

In addition, in the extraction industry, the ore may differ in thickness, depth, and grade. There are also differences in transportation conditions. In agriculture, there are differences in soil fertility and transportation conditions. These objective conditions are unalterable by subjective wishes, and they determine what the labor productivity and profit rate are.

The above reasons are often used by economists who oppose the setting of prices according to values.

But from the viewpoint of value theory, the above reservations simply demonstrate that since the law of value still exists in the socialist society, we must admit on that basis the existence of capital profit rate, production price, and differential earning (namely "differential rent"). Marx already showed in his Capital that capital profit rate, production price, and differential rent not only did not contradict the law of value, they were its logical conclusions. Marx also said that absolute rent would cease to exist after private landownership was abolished, but differential rent would continue to exist. But this "rent" or earnings should be taxed away by the state and should not be given to landlords. Although many economists admit the existence of the law of value, they still think that capital profit rate, production price, and differential rent are capitalist categories, and that they should not be used in a socialist society. Since Marx and Lenin treated differential rent at length, we will not talk about it here any more. We will talk briefly about the problem of capital profit rate and production price.

Capital profit rate and cost profit rate are two different principles of price formation. They are also different principles determining how much profit an enterprise should deliver to the state.

According to the principle of capital profit rate, the amount of profit delivered to the state by an enterprise is determined by the current average capital profit rate of the whole society. For example, if an enterprise uses 100 million yuan of capital, and the current average capital profit rate of the whole society is 20 percent, then the amount of profit that this enterprise needs to deliver to the state is 20 million yuan. If the amount of profit actually delivered to the state at the end of the year is less than this figure, this indicates that this enterprise is poorly managed and that it has not fully exploited the social capital invested in it by the state. The reasons leading to poor management must then be discovered. If the actual amount of profit sent to the state exceeds this average quota, it indicates that this enterprise is well managed. The good experience of this enterprise must then be summarized and extended.

According to the principle of capital profit rate, product prices are determined as follows: Add to the total costs of a certain product in a certain industry the total profit attributable to this product according to the capital used for its production and the average capital profit rate. The unit price of this product is the quotient from dividing this sum by the total quantity of the product. From an individual enterprise's viewpoint, the m component of the product value and the profit component of the product price are not the same. But from society's viewpoint, total m must be equal to total profit.[e]

When capital profit rate is used, enterprises which use more social capital must deliver more profit to the state. This encourages enterprises to conserve capital, especially fixed capital, and staff and workers to increase the equipment utilization rate.

But what we used in the past in many departments was not the capital profit rate but the cost profit rate borrowed from the Soviet Union in our First Five-Year Plan period. According to this system, the average profit rate of the whole society is not the average obtained by dividing total social capital into total social profit (i.e., capital profit rate), but the average obtained by dividing total costs of the total social product into the total social profit. This then is the average cost profit rate. According to this system, product price is the sum of the average cost of each product and profit calculated by the average cost profit rate. And the profit quota delivered to the state is basically the product from multiplying the total costs of the enterprise production quota by the average cost profit rate.

Under the system of cost profit rate, enterprise economic accounting actually counts only a very small portion of the total capital used by the enterprise, namely, circulating capital plus the depreciation of fixed assets. Because our depreciation period is usually twenty-five years or more (owing to accelerated technological improvement and rapid renewal of equipment, the depreciation period of the Western world has been reduced from about ten years in the nineteenth century to four to five years recently), the depreciation

e) This is the well-known transformation problem in Marx's labor theory of value. For details, see Editor's Introduction in this volume and Fundamentals of Political Economy, edited by George C. Wang and translated by K. K. Fung (White Plains, N.Y.: M. E. Sharpe, Inc., 1977), Chapter 6. — K.K.F.

charge is considerably reduced. This deflates cost and inflates profit. Consequently, only one-twenty-fifth or less of our fixed capital is included in the economic accounting of enterprises to bear the burden of profit sent to the state. Since most of the fixed assets are not accounted for, they bear no burden of profit to the state and are essentially free to the enterprises. Therefore, it is not unusual that the people in charge of enterprises want a lot of equipment and underutilize them. In the early 1960s, I asked many capable enterprise directors about the amount of circulating capital they had. They had no problem reciting the figures. But when they were asked how much fixed capital they had, none of them knew the answer. Even finance officers did not know without first looking it up in their books. Figures that are not included in economic accounting are figures that are not used. So nobody remembers what they are!

Our country lacks modern equipment. But our accounting system keeps ignoring the major portion of our total national assets in the form of fixed capital. Therefore, converting the system of cost profit rate into the system of capital profit rate should be put on the current agenda of those engaged in economic management and theoretical research.

After enterprise profit quotas delivered to the state have been determined according to the principle of capital profit rate, the advantage in labor productivity and the resulting higher profit obtained by big and foreign enterprises owing to their big and foreign equipment will be offset because more profit must be delivered on more capital. If the differential earnings from mines and farms owing to superior natural conditions are also delivered to the state through taxes, then the size of enterprise profit will depend primarily on the subjective efforts of the staff and workers in the management and operation of enterprises. Profit will become a most comprehensive indicator of enterprise performance.

8. IN RESPONSE TO THE CRITICS OF CAPITAL PROFIT RATE

As we said earlier, under the influence of dogmatic viewpoints expressed in texts on political economy, capital profit rate was in the past rejected and criticized as a capitalist economic category.

The comments of the critics can be classified into four kinds.

The first kind of criticism holds that the equalization of profit in the capitalist society is a product of capitalist competition for profit. In the socialist society the various enterprises and production departments are not allowed to compete for profit. And hence profit is not equalized. Therefore, there cannot be any average capital profit rate. This criticism applies to both the capital profit rate and the cost profit rate. Because the cost profit rate also implies an equalization of profit, the only difference is that the capital profit rate is an average profit quota based on capital used; while the cost profit rate is an average profit quota based on costs. Both are average profit. Similarly, value (average socially necessary labor), the law of value, and all quotas in the national economic plan are average figures. If this argument can be accepted, then not only will the capital profit rate be rejected, but the cost profit rate insisted on by the critics will also be rejected — so will value, the law of value, and all quotas. In the past, many economists also regarded value and the law of value as categories and laws unique to the capitalist commodity economy precisely because value and the law of value also played their roles through capitalist pursuit for profit and free competition in the capitalist commodity economy. In the capitalist commodity economy, all economic laws work through spontaneous activities. Therefore, according to the logic of the critics of capital profit rate, after people gain control of their own destiny and the capitalist commodity economy is transformed into a planned economy, all categories and laws cease to exist.

The second kind of criticism holds that value is created by labor and not by capital. Therefore, to distribute profit according to capital share is a capitalist idea. According to this criticism, only wage profit rate is proper (to distribute m according to v, i.e., to distribute what has not been distributed according to what has been distributed to live labor), and even cost profit rate is not much better capital profit rate. This is because costs include not only wage v, but also c. In other words, they include all consumption of raw materials and part of the fixed capital (depreciation charge). Therefore, cost profit rate is only an incomplete capital profit rate.

We agree that value (including profit) is created by labor, and not by capital. This is the common sense of Marxist political economy. But we cannot deny that the labor productivity in enterprises with more and foreign equipment, and higher social capital investment, is higher than that of enterprises with less and indigenous equipment, and lower social capital investment. Therefore, product cost and labor consumption in big and foreign enterprises are lower than the average cost and the average socially necessary labor. And the profit of big and foreign enterprises is necessarily greater than that of small and indigenous enterprises. This extra profit is attained by the staff and workers of big and foreign enterprises with the help of more social investment. It should therefore be attributed to the extra social investment and not to the subjective efforts of the enterprise staff and workers. Besides, let us not forget that capital in the socialist society is not the surplus value extracted by the capitalist from the worker. It is an accumulation from past labor of the working class. It is not right not to account for the higher amount of past labor accumulation used by an enterprise. The principle of free use of capital is not in the interests of the working class.

The third kind of criticism holds that the law of value consisting merely of the average socially necessary labor is sufficient for the comparison of labor productivity and investment returns for the same product among enterprises in the same industry. As to different products produced in different industries, their use values cannot be compared. The size of investment in different departments depends on public needs and people's livelihood needs, and not on investment returns. Even though the production of a certain product requires a large investment, we must still invest in it if it is necessary to satisfy public needs and people's livelihood needs. This reasoning is also correct. But there are many ways to do things. We can use "big and foreign" methods, or we can use "small and indigenous" methods. For example, there are methods which use more embodied labor and less live labor, etc. Therefore, it is necessary to undertake proper accounting no matter what projects we are talking about. The use values of different products cannot be compared. Indirectly, however, they are still comparable. Suppose we want to build two enterprises, A and B, to produce two products with different use values. If the most advanced foreign equipment is used, one billion yuan of foreign exchange is needed for each enterprise. But we only have one billion yuan of foreign exchange to import the most advanced foreign technology, and these two enterprises must be built immediately. Therefore, only one of the two enterprises can use the most up-to-date equipment. Since the two products have different use values that are not comparable, then which of the two enterprises should use imported equipment and which should use domestically produced equipment depends on how much efficiency the imported equipment can achieve. Suppose the imported equipment in enterprise A can increase efficiency by 200 percent, and the imported equipment in enterprise B can increase efficiency by 100 percent; then it is easy to see how we decide. We will let enterprise A use imported equipment and enterprise B use domestically produced equipment. It is not possible to compare two kinds of equipment and two kinds of use values. But on the point of improving labor productivity and saving capital (ultimately saving labor), comparison is possible.

The fourth kind of criticism against the capital profit rate holds that enterprises which use more fixed capital should contribute more. But the capital profit rate instead gives more money to them. What they mean is that when prices are set according to the capital profit rate, product prices will exceed values in those industries with higher organic composition of capital (industries with more big and foreign enterprises). And product prices will be below values in those industries with lower organic composition of capital (industries with more small and indigenous enterprises). This amounts to giving more money to the former and taking money away from the latter. Unfortunately, however, our critics have forgotten that our enterprises are not private enterprises of the capitalist; they are state enterprises. Their profit does not fall into the hands of any private individuals, but is delivered to the state. Therefore, production price enables big and foreign enterprises to contribute more and deliver more profit to the state. It does not give them more money. Our critics have turned the account upside down. In industries with high organic composition of capital, production efficiency is high and cost is low, leading to low product value. Conversely, in industries with low organic composition of capital, production efficiency is low and cost is high, leading to high value. Through the equalization of profit, consumers pay more for the former product and pay less for the latter product. This is very reasonable.[f]

This, then, is my response to the critics. Now there are more and more people among those engaged in practical work and theoretical research in economics who favor capital profit rate. I hope capital profit rate will be adopted as soon as possible after further discussion.

9. CAPITAL PROFIT RATE AND BONUS

When prices deviate from values, when prices are determined

f) See editor's note (e) above. — K.K.F.

according to cost profit rate, and when differential earnings in mines and farms are not taxed, to give bonus according to the size of enterprise profit would wrongly attribute to the staff and workers the extra profit resulting from state investment and superior natural conditions. But when differential earnings are deducted and profit is calculated by capital profit rate, the size of profit can separate the effects of objective conditions from those of subjective efforts. Then it is reasonable to combine bonus with extra profit. It is also in line with the principle of distribution according to labor. In fact, it is a means through which the principle of distribution according to labor can be better implemented. It facilitates the mobilization of staff and workers' activism and the promotion of production. The greater efforts of staff and workers for society should be rewarded. Under the influence of the "communist fever" fanned up by Chen Boda and Zhang Chunqiao which opposed "material incentives" and rejected the principle of distribution according to labor, I generally opposed the bonus system and profit retention in enterprises in my 1963 Profit Report. I favored delivering of all enterprise profit to the state with no retention at all. This position is wrong and detrimental to production increase. This is then my examination and self-criticism of the "Left" thinking in my 1963 Profit Report.

August 18, 1978
Jingji yanjiu [Economic Research], 1978, No. 9

Appendix

Contents of the Chinese Edition of *Some Theoretical Issues in Socialist Economics*

* Preface

* 1. Build Planning and Statistics on the Law of Value. Jingji yanjiu 1956, No. 6.

2. Classification of Producer Goods and Consumer Goods. 1957.

* 3. "Gross Output" and Related Issues. Tongji gongzuo jianbao 1956, No. 29; Tongji gongzuo 1957, No. 13.

4. Some Knowledge of Philosophy Is Necessary to Understand Economics. 1958.

5. We Must Use a Historical Perspective to Interpret Commodity Production in the Socialist Society. Jingji yanjiu 1959, No. 5.

* 6. The Role of "Value". Jingji yanjiu 1959, No. 9.

* 7. On the Financial and Economic System within the Whole People Ownership Economy. 1961.

8. On the Principle of Exchange at Equal Values and Pricing Policy. 1961.

9. Reflections on Some Theoretical Issues in Socialist Political Economy. 1961.

10. Comments on a Draft Report. 1962.

*11. An Introduction to Circulation. 1963.

12. How Economic Research Can Serve Agriculture. Jingji yanjiu 1963, No. 5.

13. The Management System of Fixed Assets and Socialist Reproduction. 1963.

14. The Profit Target in the Management System of the Socialist Planned Economy. 1963.

15. An Outline of the Speech on Production Price at the Forum on Socialist Reproduction. 1964.

16. Summary of the Speech on Production Price at the Forum on Socialist Reproduction. 1964.

17. We Must Have a Complete Understanding of Chairman Mao's Discussion on the Law of Value. Jingji yanjiu 1978, No. 11.

18. "Bourgeois Rights." 1977.

*19. Pursue Socialist Profit with Confidence. Jingji yanjiu 1978, No. 9.

20. Among All Laws, the Law of Value Is the Most Important. Guangming ribao jingjixue 1978, No. 63.

*Translated for this volume.

Index

About the Editor

A graduate of the University of Hong Kong, K. K. Fung received a Ph.D. in Economics from Harvard University. In 1964-65 he taught at the Chinese University of Hong Kong, in 1970-75 he taught at Victoria University in Wellington, New Zealand, and since 1975 he has been on the faculty of Memphis State University where he is now an associate professor of economics.

The author of numerous articles on economics in general and the Chinese economy in particular, Dr. Fung is the translator of Fundamentals of Political Economy (1977), Chinese Economic Planning (1978), the editor and translator of Xue Muqiao, Current Economic Problems in China (1982), and for several years he served as the chief translator of Chinese Economic Studies, a journal of translations.

For Product Safety Concerns and Information please contact our EU
representative GPSR@taylorandfrancis.com
Taylor & Francis Verlag GmbH, Kaufingerstraße 24, 80331 München, Germany

www.ingramcontent.com/pod-product-compliance
Ingram Content Group UK Ltd.
Pitfield, Milton Keynes, MK11 3LW, UK
UKHW022124190926
475702UK00013B/1633